The Secret History of the Jersey Devil

THE

SECRET HISTORY
of the JERSEY DEVIL

*How Quakers, Hucksters, and Benjamin Franklin
Created a Monster*

Brian Regal
Frank J. Esposito

Kean University

JOHNS HOPKINS UNIVERSITY PRESS
Baltimore

Johns Hopkins University Press
2715 North Charles Street
Baltimore, Maryland 21218-4363
www.press.jhu.edu

Library of Congress Cataloging-in-Publication Data

Names: Regal, Brian, author. | Esposito, Frank J., author.
Title: The secret history of the Jersey Devil : how Quakers, hucksters,
    and Benjamin Franklin created a monster / Brian Regal, Frank J.
    Esposito.
Description: Baltimore : Johns Hopkins University Press, 2018. |
    Includes bibliographical references and index.
Identifiers: LCCN 2017030369| ISBN 9781421424897 (hardcover :
    alk. paper) | ISBN 1421424894 (hardcover : alk. paper) | ISBN
    9781421424910 (electronic) |ISBN 1421424916 (electronic)
Subjects: LCSH: Jersey Devil (Monster) | Legends—New Jersey—Pine
    Barrens. | Monsters—New Jersey—Pine Barrens. | Folklore—New
    Jersey—Pine Barrens. | New Jersey—Politics and government—To
    1775. | New Jersey—Church history—18th century. | United
    States—Politics and government—To 1775. | United States—Church
    history—18th century. | BISAC: HISTORY / United States /
    Colonial Period (1600–1775). | HISTORY / United States / State
    & Local / Middle Atlantic (DC, DE, MD, NJ, NY, PA). | SOCIAL
    SCIENCE / Folklore & Mythology.
Classification: LCC GR110.N5 R45 2018 | DDC 398.209749/48—
    dc23
LC record available at https://lccn.loc.gov/2017030369

A catalog record for this book is available from the British Library.

Frontispiece: A very Jersey Devil–like creature, Monstrum alatum, from
Ulisse Aldrovandi, *Monstrorum Historia* (Nicolai Tebaldine, 1642). This
image can also be found in Gaspar Schott's *Physica Curiosa* (1697).

Special discounts are available for bulk purchases of this book.
For more information, please contact Special Sales at 410-516-6936 or
specialsales@press.jhu.edu.

Johns Hopkins University Press uses environmentally friendly book
materials, including recycled text paper that is composed of at least
30 percent post-consumer waste, whenever possible.

To my mother, Elizabeth, who taught me the importance of reading; my sister, Celeste, who showed me what an artist was; and my father, Henry, who always supported my offbeat life goals and believed, as a construction worker with barely a high school education, that two marks of success were being able to wear a tie to work and living in a house on a street with no sidewalks. And as always, thanks to Lisa.

BRIAN REGAL

To Alexandra, Ella, Henry, and George, my grandchildren, who inspire me to investigate life's legends, mysteries, and monsters in order to answer their fascinating questions.

FRANK J. ESPOSITO

Contents

Acknowledgments

It can be a touchy thing when professional historians enter a world dominated by amateurs and passionate aficionados. The amateurs often look with disdain upon the interloping professionals, fearing they are there to undermine their work or to snatch it away and drag their efforts off to the ivory tower without giving the amateurs their due. Amateurs, however, deserve respect. They can focus on excruciating minutia of local history in ways professional scholars are rarely able or inclined to do. In the case of the story of the Jersey Devil, a number of hardworking and persistent local historians have unearthed much information we have made use of here.

We would like to thank Norman Goos and other members of the Atlantic County area chapter of the Sons of the American Revolution. B. K. Giberson graciously commented on part of the manuscript and helped clear up a number of tangled issues. Everett Leeds, of England, led us to some records there. Fr. J. Conner Haynes of St. Mary's Church, Burlington, did an enthusiastic search of church records for Leeds materials, and his knowledge of church history greatly assisted us. Thanks to Blake Smith for allowing Brian Regal to come on his show, *Monster Talk*, to chat about the Jersey Devil.

We would also like to thank several people who read drafts of the text in various stages. The comments of Mark Lender, Terry Golway, and Sharon Hill proved extremely useful. The librarians at the Kean University Library; Mary Beth Ortzman and Dale Lonkart of the Atlantic County Historical Society; librarians at the Burlington County Historical Society; Jacinda Williams of the Camden County Historical Society; and librarians and archivists at the Library of Congress, the New York Public Library, the Kearny Public Library, the Newark Public Library, Sinclair Special Collections, Rutgers University, the New Jersey Historical Society, the Bodleian Library, Oxford, and the British Library and the Library of the Society of Friends, both of London, did what great librarians do by helping locate obscure, hard-to-find materials in their collections.

Thanks to Mr. Timothy Duke of the Royal College of Arms, London, for help with questions about the Leeds family crest. We are especially appreciative of the assistance of Angus K. Gillespie of Rutgers University. Thanks to the Kean University Foundation, for supplying funding that allowed this research to go forward, and to our outstanding colleagues in the Kean University Department of History, who showed great patience and support for our project about a monster.

We are also indebted to Mark Lender for sage advice as this book was being written. A special note of appreciation also goes to Daniel Paul Graifman for his enthusiasm, support, and valuable suggestions regarding the story of the Jersey Devil.

Also, thanks to everyone at Johns Hopkins University Press for their efforts, and to the anonymous reviewers who made suggestions and caught little errors that made the final book that much better. In the end, any factual errors are ours.

The Secret History of the Jersey Devil

INTRODUCTION

Hell is empty and all the devils are here.—Shakespeare, *The Tempest*

ON A COLD LATE AFTERNOON in January of 1929, a posse of armed men moved cautiously through the woods of southern New Jersey, near Leeds Point and the Atlantic Ocean. They were chasing a fugitive who had frightened the local population and left footprints in the snow that confirmed his presence. Horrendous tales of this interloper's misdeeds had circulated widely, but were dismissed by local authorities, and so the searchers determined to put a stop to it once and for all on their own. Like the torch- and pitchfork-wielding villagers from *Frankenstein*, this mob pursued a monster. They thought they were on the trail of the Jersey Devil.

The Jersey Devil, supposedly a nightmarish beast inhabiting the forests of the state from which it gets its name, appears as a kind of debased and deformed flying horse with glowing red eyes. It has been sighted often over the years, and there are claims that it has done terrible things and presaged catastrophes. Believers claim it is the result of a liaison between a woman and the devil. Legends about its ghostly antics have been advanced and enhanced in movies, television, comic books, and cyberspace.

Everything you think you know about the Jersey Devil, however, is wrong. The real story of the Jersey Devil's birth is far more interesting, complex, and important than most people realize. The search for the Jersey Devil is not a pursuit of monsters, but the search for ghosts: the ghosts of early New Jersey and, more broadly, early America. These ghosts are not disembodied spirits; they are the ephemeral memories of people whose lives have been lost to the past. The story concerns real people with real issues of religion, politics, citizenship, and social allegiances. It turned into a tale of credulity, mythmaking, and fear of the unknown.

Much time and energy have been invested in promoting the legend of the Jersey Devil, in trying to discover the "monster" and in proving it real. This book is an attempt to trace the origins of the legend to its source and to clear away the layers of fancies, fallacies, hoaxes, and half-remembered confabulations to get to the story's heart. In this way we can get a glimpse into not only the origins of a legend but also the origins of a nation.

What lifts this local monster legend out of provincial obscurity is its unappreciated roots in the early days of North American colonization and its place in the founding of both the state of New Jersey and the United States. The Jersey Devil began its life as the Leeds Devil, a political animal. The only thing reliable about the traditional story of the Jersey Devil is its association with the Leeds family. They were pioneers who published the first almanacs and books in the colony of New Jersey. Daniel Leeds, the family patriarch, was erudite and politically and religiously active, and he helped shape modern American political culture in profound ways. Had he lived a generation later, we might speak of him as one of the Founding Fathers. He intended to bring the Scientific Revolution to the New World, and several of his descendants fought with distinction in the American Revolution. One helped found Atlantic City; another was its first mayor. The Leeds family helped forge a nation. Yet despite this place in history, the Leedses are all but forgotten today, except by their descendants and a small band of intrepid genealogists. Worse still, memories of them as well as the family's reputation have been distorted by stories of monsters and figures of the occult.

In the twenty-first century there are many aficionados of the Jersey Devil. A quick search of the internet will reveal a legion of sites where stories are discussed and examined. Groups regularly go out into the Pine Barrens to look for the creature. They arm themselves with motion detectors, infrared cameras, and other tools of the modern monster-hunting trade. They hope to one day bring in physical evidence of the Devil's existence. Their giddy persistence keeps the story alive but also masks its origins. The element that most undermines the efforts of monster enthusiasts is that the story of the Jersey Devil has nothing to do with evil witches or leathery winged beasts haunting the woods. There is no living creature. This is not the story of the fictional birth of a monster, but of the life of a man.

DANIEL LEEDS (1652–1720) came to the New World in the late 1670s and settled in Burlington, in what was then West Jersey, an area dominated by religious dissenters known as the Society of Friends, also called Quakers. A Quaker himself, Leeds published an almanac and was promptly attacked by his neighbors over his use of astrology in it. He followed the almanac with a grand book of metaphysical philosophy. His neighbors burned that book as heretical to their Christian belief system. Disillusioned by his treatment, he satirized his fellow Quakers in a series of stinging and sarcastic exposés on colonial life. He set himself up as an independent thinker. With an attitude in tune with the burgeoning Age of Enlightenment, he determined to "set a resolution to search and try things for [him]self, and not believe on trust or because others did."[1] His work constitutes the earliest publishing in the region. Building upon a British tradition, the feuds he engaged in included some of the earliest political attack literature produced in America, which helped lay the groundwork for today's innuendo- and scandal-laden journalism, with its focus on hearsay and rumor rather than facts. His accusations of misdeeds of the Quaker majority so outraged the Friends that they accused him of working for the devil, and so they labeled Leeds as "Satan's Harbinger." To make matters worse, Leeds supported the first royal governor of New Jersey, the infamous Lord Cornbury: a man accused of being loose with colony taxes and a cross-dresser. Eventually, one of Daniel's many sons, Titan Leeds, took over running the almanac and ran squarely into a young man named Benjamin Franklin. The upstart Franklin was then angling to make a name for himself as a publisher. As a publicity stunt, Franklin—in the guise of "Poor Richard" Saunders—claimed that astrological calculations showed that his publishing rival Titan Leeds would die in 1733. When the prediction did not pan out, Leeds proclaimed Franklin a fool and a liar. Never missing a beat, Franklin claimed that, since Titan Leeds had died, his ghost must be out to get him. Leeds tried to defend himself, but Franklin kept a straight face and argued that Leeds had been resurrected from the dead. Thus *Poor Richard's Almanac* became famous while the *Leeds Almanac* dwindled and disappeared.

The trail of Daniel Leeds moves from his birth in England through his life in the Pine Barrens, chronicling his rise to prominence in his community, his publication of the earliest printed tracts in the region, his chastisement at the hands of his neighbors for those publications, his resistance to censorship, his part in the creation of a new type of political literature, his place in the Scientific Revolution, the rise of his son, and his family's eventual disappearance into the mists of time. It also covers his transformation into a monster. The trail snakes through the printed materials of a time of precarious living and of hard work building a society in a wilderness, of passionate religious feeling, of the dawning of science as an arbiter of knowledge, and of growing nationalism and pride—a time of human adventure.

Complicating the matter, there are two Devil stories here. The first concerns the foundational events upon which the story originally began—the actual people involved and how they came to be associated with the story. The second is how the legend, once divorced from its original sources, came to dominate the notion of the myth. The majority of current literature on the Jersey Devil legend is profoundly misleading. An army of "investigators," monster hunters, and authors on cryptozoology have propagated a legend they think is somehow real, having no idea of its origins or how it was created in the first place. The Jersey Devil lurks, not in the woods, but in the library. Years of internet embellishment, particularly concerning the Jersey Devil hysteria of 1909, often without checking on original sources or looking wider afield for archival material, has added fresh layers of unnecessary obscurity and unfounded speculation. This study seeks to rescue the facts from memory and to take once-real figures that had become fictive and make them real again.

THIS BOOK IS LAID OUT in two major parts. The first half tells the story of the little-known origins of the Leeds Devil, as the creature was originally known. In chapter 1 we address the colonial background of the story. In chapter 2 we examine the life of the primary character in the drama, Daniel Leeds, and the world he lived in: the world of colonial New Jersey during the Enlightenment, on the eve of the American Revolution. This is crucial to understanding how his name, and the name of the wider Leeds family, became associated with the myth. Chapter 3 is the story of Leeds's son, Titan, and, notably, his feud with Benjamin Franklin. This becomes the foundation upon which the second story, that of the Jersey Devil, can be built. In chapter 4 we explain how the current mythos comes out of tabloid newspaper accounts and a general loss of memory about the previous part of the story. Here we also lay out the long history of beliefs in monsters and other strange occurrences that permeated American culture in the nineteenth century. This material makes it easier to understand how the Jersey Devil legend could have become so well known, so popular, and so quickly accepted. Chapter 5 shows how the belief in the Jersey Devil came to be propagated by a cadre of amateur history writers. Finally, in chapter 6, fueled by modern media in the later twentieth century, the Jersey Devil becomes a star.

The Jersey Devil is not just a local monster story or some provincial tall tale with little relevance or interest to the outside world. In this case the story illuminates a forgotten chapter in American history. It is a story involving national origins, religious bigotry, land grabs, and failed intellectual pursuits. It is also the story of a father-and-son tragedy of almost Shakespearian proportions.

Remembering the past involves the search for identity, and so stories are told. These help us to remember, but they can also help us to forget. Stories can obscure the past, hide events, and transform heroes into villains and villains into heroes. They can teach moral lessons and warn us of the future. Stories celebrate ancestors and disparage them. They can take humans and turn them into monsters.

CHAPTER ONE

"Let this one be a Devil!"

T HE JERSEY DEVIL ranks as the most popular legend in the folklore
of the Garden State and is one of the oldest in the United States. It
is widely known around the world. Several versions of the legend
exist, all sharing a central narrative. In 1735, a witch known as Mother
Leeds found herself pregnant for the thirteenth time. Breeching, she called
out in agony, "Oh, let this one be a devil!" The child then either emerged
with, or soon developed, a horse-like head, bat-like wings, claws, and hooves.
The creature yelped menacingly at the horrified family, then flew up the
chimney and off into the forest, where it spent the next several centuries
harassing and attacking unfortunate travelers.[1]

Mother Leeds makes no attempt to love or nurture her offspring and,
rather than mourn his loss, is relieved to be rid of him. It is the female—a
self-centered, uncaring, unloving mother—who bears the brunt of the blame.
She becomes a scapegoat for various fears about witches, non-Christians,
and women in general. She is an outsider, rural, uneducated, and prone to
supernatural and superstitious beliefs and who has sex with the devil. Some
versions of the story have her curse the child in the process of being born,
while some have her make the curse before the child is even conceived.

A version recounted by folklorist John McPhee has Mother Leeds as an
even more reprehensible character, who first curses a "preacher" who tries to
convert her. It is unclear what denomination he is trying to convert her to,
or what religion she is following that the preacher felt it necessary to convert
her. In this version it is the preacher who curses Mother Leeds so that her
next child will be the spawn of the Devil. The hideous beast is born, but lives
with its parents until the age of four. It then kills both parents and heads off
into the woods.[2] Regardless of the version of the story, Mother Leeds never
comes out well. Her offspring, however, fares even worse.

The Jersey Devil itself has little development as a character. The only
details of its life and behavior occur within the confines of the Leeds home.
The legend tells the circumstances of its birth, something of its physical
appearance and morphology, and its mode of locomotion. It does not speak,
but only yelps once at the stunned crowd of onlookers.

Along with being a commentary on colonial American life, the Jersey

Devil myth is a window into the treatment of the indigenous Lenape people. Once filled with Native legends of forest dragons, the Pine Barrens had its supernatural inhabitants reduced to a single Anglo-American entity. Not only are the Lenape people of the region ousted from their lands, so are their spirits and monsters. The Jersey Devil's transformation is thus also an ethnic one: its Lenape heritage filtered out and forgotten. Today's legend, as told, has no Native elements. It occurs wholly outside the Native experience, as if that had never existed, despite its connections.

The colonial American world of the Jersey Devil's conception was a place of multicultural interaction. Newly arriving European refugees and immigrants jostled, sometimes peacefully, sometimes violently, with one another and with the Native people. In this tapestry of cultural beliefs, aspirations, resentments, and trepidations, the various parts of the Jersey Devil's strange anatomy would be sewn together from disparate sources. This slow process of assemblage is what allowed the legend to take flight.

Life in the Jerseys

Europeans first began to become aware of what would become New Jersey when Giovanni da Verrazano sailed past in 1524 and Henry Hudson explored the coast in 1609. The earliest settlers came in the 1620s, from Holland and Sweden, but not in large numbers. Parts of the region came to be known variously as New Netherlands, then New Sweden, and also Nova-Caeseria.[3] By 1664 this land had come under the control of the English. In 1673 the Dutch briefly recaptured New Netherlands, including the area of present-day northern New Jersey, Staten Island, and New York City. A British fleet arrived on the scene, and the Dutch governor, Peter Stuyvesant, had little choice but to relinquish control. The Treaty of Westminster put all the territory under the British crown. New York, New Jersey, and the rest of the colonies remained British until the Revolution.

Following the English takeover, George Carteret (1610–80) and Lord John Berkeley received the land between the Hudson River south to the Delaware River as royal presents. Carteret received this largesse for having protected the future Charles II during the English Civil War. As Carteret hailed from the island of Jersey in the English Channel, it became New Jersey. The region was divided into East Jersey, the area bordering the Hudson, and West Jersey, bordering the Delaware. Eventually Carteret and Berkeley sold their interests in these separate provinces to two groups of ambitious religionists known as the Society of Friends, also called Quakers, who were looking for a place to make a home free of persecution. Through a series of deals and complex maneuverings, the well-known Quaker William Penn, who already had an interest in West Jersey, also acquired control over lands west of the Delaware that would become known as Pennsylvania.

West Jersey was heavily forested with conifers of many different species. In the geological past, the Atlantic Ocean had extended inland as far west as modern-day Philadelphia. When the ocean eventually receded, it left the region a flat, sandy, coastal plain. The more thickly forested parts remained relatively uninhabited into the twenty-first century. Summers could be oppressively hot, while winters regularly saw heavy snowfall. The Pine Barrens, as the region came to be known, did have one major advantage to recommend it: the Delaware River could be entered directly from the Atlantic Ocean and was navigable by large ships, making access to the interior easy. Gabriel Thomas, in his 1698 book about Pennsylvania and West Jersey, noted that the Native people living in the region had quite nice dispositions. The Indians, Thomas said, "are suppos'd by most [European] people to have been of the Ten Scattered Tribes, for they resemble the Jews very much."[4] It was largely available land, low population, and accessibility to water traffic that attracted William Penn and the Quakers.

Born of the upheavals of the English Civil Wars, in 1647 a group of religious dissenters formed a new sect they called the Society of Friends. Because they claimed to shake with the inner light of the Lord, they became commonly known as Quakers. They believed an individual need not have a priest or clergyman or other official between them and God. The connection with the divine came through an individual's direct relationship with Jesus. They rejected worldly things, as well. It was not uncommon for individual Quakers to walk down the street naked except for a dish over their private areas, or to walk into churches loudly exclaiming for people to reject earthly authority and seek God directly. This public behavior, seen by others as scandalous, brought them into conflict first, with the Cromwellian parliamentary government, and after the Restoration, with the Crown.

The Quakers also found themselves at odds with the Puritans of England, who considered the Quakers heretics. The Puritans felt that the Protestant Reformation had not gone far enough for their liking. They viewed the Anglican majority as still essentially Catholics—a group the Puritans despised. They wanted to purify the church to bring it more in line with their view of the ideals of the Reformation. As time went by, the Puritans grew in number and political power. They wanted to set their version of Anglicanism up as the state religion. When that did not quite work out in England, some Puritans headed to the Boston area of North America with the dream of setting up a Puritan stronghold there: a place they called New England. Once established, they took control of local politics and religion and began to persecute anyone they deemed heretical.

Seeking to flee Puritan persecution in England, beginning in 1656, many Quakers removed to Massachusetts, only to find grief at the hands of Puritans there. The Puritans resisted the Quakers' desire to practice their faith openly and freely.[5] The Puritans disliked the Quaker rejection of authority and the preacher class, their support of women's equality as well as that of the Native people, and their rejection of worldly possessions. The Puritan government in Boston passed various anti-Quaker laws, which had fines and bodily maiming as punishments. Some of the first Quakers to arrive— Mary Fisher and Ann Austin—were tried and imprisoned; some Quakers were executed.

While a few Quakers made the decision to stay in Boston and fight, others headed south. They swarmed into West Jersey, quickly outnumbering the few Dutch and Swedes already there. Along with the Friends, Catholics and Anglicans also found their way to the region. Unlike in Massachusetts, where religion formed the basis for local government, there was little outward confrontation between these groups in Eastern Pennsylvania and West Jersey. In West Jersey, Quaker communities, farms, and meeting houses appeared from the Atlantic Ocean to the Delaware River.[6] Quakers back in England soon began coming to West Jersey to settle. One of those families was named Leeds.

Few cultures exist in complete isolation from others. The Quakers had fled persecution at the hands of the Puritans, but when they arrived in the Jerseys they still encountered other groups. The Native people of the region, known as the Lenape, did not threaten or persecute the Quakers. In turn, the Quakers did not persecute the Lenape. The Quakers had an unusually progressive attitude to their Native neighbors and were one of the first Anglo-American groups to fight for the equal rights of the Native people (later they were staunch abolitionists). The Lenape still had an important, but subtle, impact upon the Quakers, particularly their religious beliefs about forest beings and supposed Native American evil powers.

Native American Elements

The Jersey Devil may be the oldest Anglo-American monster legend in North American history; to Native Americans, however, the Jersey Devil was a latecomer. The Lenape people, who inhabited the region long before the advent of Europeans, already had a pantheon of forest spirits with narratives to go with them. In order to more fully understand the formation of

This map shows seventeenth-century European settlements of what would become New Jersey. The area surrounding New York City is East Jersey; the region along the Delaware River is West Jersey. New Jersey Historical Commission / Peter O. Wacker

the Jersey Devil legend, Native American belief systems must be taken into account. Lenape ideas about monsters melded with and influenced how the Jersey Devil legend was constructed by later Anglo-Americans.

Native people understood the elements of weather, environmental changes, and the world around them by creating a system of spiritual beliefs that explained life's events. As a deeply spiritual people, Native Americans saw everything in the world as being due to the actions of a supreme guiding spirit. Europeans similarly interpreted what they encountered in the New World within the framework of their own predominantly Christian beliefs. As a result, the Lenape and the Quakers, at least, had many points of similarity and an easy sympathy in their metaphysical views on nature.[7] Not all Christians viewed Native American religions in the same understanding ways.

The creation of the Jersey Devil story has its roots in the cultural, religious, and political beliefs of both European colonists and the Native Lenape Indians who lived in the Jerseys. Europeans arrived in the Americas expecting that wild beings and strange beasts populated its deepest forests. In encountering the vast region of pines of western New Jersey, the early colonists must have been in awe of the place. At the time of first European-Lenape contact, the pinelands extended from where Asbury Park is now, south to Cape May, and from the Atlantic Ocean west to the Delaware River.[8]

Early relations between the Lenape and the Dutch and the Swedes, and their fur-trading colonies of New Netherlands (1624) and New Sweden (1638) and the later English colony of New Jersey (1664), brought about the early creation of a widespread belief among European-Americans that the Lenape were "devil-worshipping savages." As early as 1633, when John De-Laet's *New World* was published in Europe, promotional and descriptive literature promulgated this view. DeLaet wrote that the Indians of New Netherlands "have no worship of God; they indeed pay homage to the Devil, but not so solemnly nor with such precise ceremonies as the Africans do."[9] This inaccurate description enabled the early non-Quaker colonists to justify their commercial exploitation of the Indians and, in time of conflict, to kill them. In New Netherlands, Willhelm Kieft, the Dutch colonial governor, even provided that a bounty be paid for the scalps of the Raritan-Lenape Indians. Later relations with the Quakers would be far less antagonistic.

For many Europeans the Pine Barren's dense vegetation, its strange, even bizarre, carnivorous plants and unusual animals—such as the giant Sand Crane—as well as the overpowering quietude all contributed to a sense of looming danger. Even today, many of those who venture into the deepest recesses of the Pine Barrens report similar feelings of foreboding. Europeans were thus susceptible to the stories they learned from the Native people about life in the Pine Barrens. They were also likely intrigued by Lenape ceremonies honoring their forest god known as M'sing.[10] Indians described this important deity as a deer-like creature with leathery wings or a deer being ridden by a man.[11] M'Sing has frequently been depicted as being similar to ("deer-like creature with wings") descriptions of the Jersey Devil throughout New Jersey history. These similarities can be seen as an example of cultural transmission of a story between European colonists and the Lenape based on the fears of both Indians and colonists regarding the surrounding forest.

The idea of forest spirits resonated with the two cultures. Later writers tended to exaggerate these fears. As folklorist Henry Charlton Beck warned in quoting from a 1905 article by J. Elfreth Watkins called "On the Trail of the Jersey Devil": "There tapers up from its deep base along the Delaware Bay to its apex at Long Branch a green triangle known as 'the Pines.' Its black, innermost heart has suffered a hiatus, a quick transition from twentieth to eighteenth century, plunged into a dark, sylvan realm of witches, conjurors and monsters."[12] One of the most famous descriptions of the Leeds Devil, since established as spurious, comes from the supposed 1790 diary entry of a woodsman named Vance Larner:

> It was neither beast, nor man, nor spirit, but a hellish brew of all three. It was beside a pond when I came upon it. I stopped and it did not move. Nay, I could not move. It was dashing its tail to and fro in the pond and rubbing its horns against a tree trunk. It was as large as a moose with leather wings. It had cloven hooves as big around as an oak's trunk. After it was through with the tree, it yielded an awful scream as if it were a pained man, and then flew across the pond until I could see it no more.[13]

To the precontact Lenape Indians there was no such entity as the "Devil," or "Satan." This represented a completely unknown idea until they heard European colonists launch religious sermons aimed at converting them and saving them from the Devil. They held no belief in the powers of a Devil in the Christian sense until after contact with the Europeans. However, they did think that both good and evil spirits existed in the world. They hoped that by paying homage, through prayers and ceremonies directed to the good spirits, they could maintain a balance against evil people or the bad spirits that controlled them.

An all-powerful god, sometimes called "Manito," or "Kishelemukong," was able to control all things in the world, but the Lenape did not see him as the embodiment of evil.[14] Although the Lenape took careful precautions against evil spirits, they did not believe these evil tendencies were embodied in a single entity. Evil spirits alone represented enough of a threat to their well-being, and it was thought they could be anywhere. For instance, the Lenape made holes in the soles of a baby's moccasins in order to let any evil spirits escape from the body of the infant. Even in the mid-twentieth century, Lenape (Delaware) Indian children in Oklahoma were told not to whistle at night for fear the activity would attract evil spirits.[15]

In describing the Lenape reaction to the power of lightning, Peter Lindstrom, a Swedish architect who visited the colony of New Sweden in the 1650s, wrote that "the savages are so frightened that they hide themselves . . .

for they know that the evil one exists, who can send them that which is evil."[16] Like so many seventeenth- and eighteenth-century writers, Lindstrom confuses the Indians' fear of the power of their gods, especially the all-powerful Manito, or Kishelemukong, with a fear of a devil, or of Satan. This is a typical mistake found in the descriptions of European observers at that time. Lindstrom laments that the Natives would not believe, or understand, that "there is an almighty and good God who can do them every good."[17] Lindstrom and other early writers also see the use of the carved amulets that represent the personal guardian spirits of the Lenape as being an example of devil worship. In reality, these Manitowuk are representative of Indian belief in the power of each Indian's protective guardian spirit. The amulet was fashioned after a representation of the spirit seen, or dreamt of, during puberty rituals. The amulet was then worn as a necklace, with the creature's face to the wearer so that it could watch and protect the wearer. To someone standing in front of the wearer, it would appear that the face was upside down. The amulet was powerful enough to protect the owner from evil spirits, so other people were not permitted to touch it.[18]

It appears likely that the Europeans took the Lenape description of M'sing and made it into a devil by applying a Christian interpretation to it.[19] The colonists heard many stories about M'Sing and saw the Lenape Indians pay homage to it in ceremonies. After leaving New Jersey, the Lenape in Copan, Oklahoma, as recently as 1924, were still performing these rituals. The "Big House Ceremony," as it was then called, was a derivative of the Gamwing harvest ceremony once celebrated in the Pine Barrens.[20] The colonists melded the description of M'Sing with the Christian concept of Lucifer. The dangerous and forbidding Pine Barrens seemed an ideal place to European settlers for such a creature to inhabit.

A creature vaguely resembling the description of the Jersey Devil existed in prehistoric North America and is known from the fossil record. An Ice Age impala-like animal called *Tarsus Pterodactyl* existed and became extinct after the retreat of the Wisconsin glacier, more than 11,000 years ago.[21] A few writers have speculated that this creature might have ended up in the New Jersey region by being pushed just ahead of the glacier. The glacier's terminal moraine, or southernmost extension, crossed what is now Perth Amboy, on the east, to Belvidere on the west.[22] That would put the creature's likely place of escape from the massive ice squarely in the Pine Barrens. However, no known remains identified as *Tarsus Pterodactyl* have yet been found in New Jersey.[23] The remains of an alleged "Jersey Devil" found in 1957, after a forest fire in the Wharton State Forest section of the Pine

Barrens, were apparently never scientifically studied and their whereabouts is presently unknown. Photographs do exist of the burned remains of what newspapers at that time called a "monster." This story will be discussed in detail later.[24]

The Pine Barrens of New Jersey therefore present an ideal setting for the Jersey Devil story. For many years scholars of the Lenape people thought there were few Indian habitation sites there, but more recent archaeological researchers have shown that the Lenape inhabited the pines in greater numbers than previously thought. Archaeologists John Cavallo, Richard Regensburg, and others excavated Indian settlements in the heart of the region and uncovered many former hamlets and campsites.[25] It is likely, given their worship of M'sing as the guardian of the creatures within it, that the Lenape viewed the pinelands as a sacred place. For them, the importance of the pinelands was clearly linked to their all-encompassing religious belief that every natural element held spiritual significance, including the weather, the earth, the trees, the animals. They also believed, as did most colonial-era Christians, that humans too could manipulate the environment through occult means.

Devils and Witches

Colonists not only in New England but also in New Jersey were obsessed with witchcraft and monsters. Stories abounded in eighteenth-century New Jersey that witches as well as Satan himself operated in the Pine Barrens. One popular tale centered on a "Witch of the Pines," who would stop wayward travelers and cast a spell on them. At the heart of the Jersey Devil story is a witch named Mother Leeds.

In May of 1668 fear of witches in East Jersey led the General Assembly to pass a law that stated, "If any person be found to be a witch, either male or female[,] they shall be put to death."[26] The assembly reenacted the law again in 1675. There is a court case in East Jersey records involving the litigation of Abigail Sharp against Abraham Shotwell. Although no final disposition of the lawsuit has been found, the case is fascinating because Shotwell maintained that he saw Sharp return from "flying all night" and "saw her land in a patch of beans" before seeing her in "the shape of a cat on the top of his house."[27] She responded that she was innocent of any occult activity and that he was lying to ruin her good name.

A story written by Benjamin Franklin may have contributed to the story of Mother Leeds's devilish child. Entitled "A Witch Trial at Mt. Holly," it purported to be an account of the trial of an alleged witch in New Jersey.

Franklin, then one of the owners of the *Pennsylvania Gazette*, anonymously wrote this satire to ridicule the silliness of witch hunting:

> It seems the accused had been charged with making their Neighbors Sheep dance in an uncommon manner, and with causing Hogs to speak, and sing Psalms, &c. to the great Terror and Amazement of the King's good and peaceable subjects in this Province; and the Accusers being very positive that if the accused were weighed in Scales against a Bible, the Bible would prove too heavy for them; or that, if they were bound and put into the River, they would swim; the said accused desirous to make their innocence appear, voluntarily offered to undergo said Trials, if 2 of the most violent of their Accusers would be tried with them.[28]

When the scales were loaded with a Bible on one side and a rather large accused wizard, or male witch, on the other, the spectators expressed great surprise that "flesh and bones" of the alleged wizard outweighed "the great good Book." In their book *The Jersey Devil* (1976), James F. McCloy and Ray Miller speculated that Franklin's fictional story might have started a then-widespread belief that a devil child was born in the pines near Mount Holly.[29]

Like the Puritans and other European settlers to the New World, the Lenape Indians believed that witches existed and that they could conjure spells and perform evil deeds. They believed that witches lived in remote forested areas and that they could fly. The Lenape believed witches could thereby travel great distances at night. They called them Kimochene, or nightwalkers.[30] The Kimochene were humans inhabiting the bodies of evil creatures.

So pronounced were these fears of evil spirits that the Lenape, by then called *Delaware*, practiced even into the twentieth century the technique of "chinking," which is the use of moss and clay to fill the cracks in the space between logs used to build their homes. The anthropologist Frank Speck noted that this was done to prevent witches from slipping into their homes.[31] Speck's work among the Lenape-Delaware in Oklahoma in the twentieth century examines carefully the Indians' witchcraft beliefs and traditions. Speck wrote of the Delaware, "One of the last of the Delaware witches is said to have joined the church, but continued to practice witchcraft. She believed that she could not find salvation because she had sold her soul to the Devil, but by joining the Church, thought she could secure some peace of mind."[32] By then the Indians were well aware of the enticements of the Christian devil. The unique combination of colonial and Indian fears of witches, when combined with Lenape Indian religious traditions, especially that of M'sing— the god protecting the forest animals—contributed to the groundwork that would allow for the creation of first the Leeds Devil and then the Jersey Devil. Alongside these spiritual beliefs came old-fashioned political intrigues.

Along with Native American legends and European transplant stories, there is one other possible source of the Jersey Devil myth: a monstrous birth born to the Leeds family. Monstrous births, such as babies with two heads, multiple arms and legs or no arms or legs, both fascinated and repulsed Europeans and became the source for a considerable and popular printed literature.[33] Pamphlets and broadsides on monstrous births, often accompanied by lurid illustrations alternately accurate or outrageously fantastic, sold well, particularly in England, whence many early settlers of New Jersey hailed. Along with depicting actual births of deformed animals and humans, monster pamphlets used such cases as excuses to attack political or religious groups. Attaching a monster to a religious denomination, an individual, or a family proved an effective way to bring social ridicule upon the target.[34] Fortunately for religious bigots, one existed in colonial America.

The Curious Case of Anne Hutchinson

Whereas the story of Mother Leeds and her monster child is fictional, there was a real woman who, in broad outlines, resembles her. Anne Hutchinson was an important early political and religious radical in the Massachusetts Bay Colony. In the city of Boston, Hutchinson (1591–1643) fought vociferously against the ruling Puritan elites of the 1630s and '40s. As part of the Antinomian Controversy, Hutchinson and others felt that the Puritan idea of the Covenant of Works was not enough to ensure salvation; one had to hear the spirit of the Lord on a personal level in order to ultimately achieve Free Grace. She also questioned the right of the clergy class to be the intercessors between an individual and God (thus assuring the clergy's leadership and control). Her outspoken behavior and defiance of the ruling Puritan class made her a pariah. Arrested and tried for heresy, Hutchinson found herself banished from Boston. She and a number of followers left to take up residence in the more tolerant city of Providence, Rhode Island.[35] At about this time Hutchinson became pregnant for the sixteenth time. She gave birth to a disturbing mass that bore little resemblance to a child.[36] Just before this, one of her young protégés, Mary Dyer (1611–60), had also given birth to a deformed child (Mary would later be executed by the Puritans because, among other things, she had converted to Quakerism).

With the tales of the lives of Anne Hutchinson and Mary Dyer, colonial America had stories of women who, because of their independence, strong will, and resistance to church domination, had suffered the wrath of God by being made to produce monsters. Just as in the European monster story tra-

Anne Hutchinson, the Puritan rebel. Already disliked by the Boston clergy, when she gave birth to a monstrous child she was condemned as a heretic. She could have been a model for "Mother Leeds."

ditions, Anne Hutchinson earned her dilemma, her monstrous child, as punishment for her supposedly un-Christian and antisocial behavior. That she had given birth to a monster was just one more reason to consider her a heretic in need of cleansing from the community. Puritan clergy used these monstrous births to frighten their parishioners into proper behavior and as examples of what God would do to the unrighteous. (Seemingly adding to her guilt, Anne Hutchinson later perished in Connecticut at the hands of Native people who were retaliating for their own persecution at the hands of Christians.)[37] The governor of Massachusetts, John Winthrop, commented publically on both Anne Hutchinson and Mary Dyer.[38] The cautionary tale of an out-of-control woman of dubious religiosity giving birth to a beast, already common in European circles, was also part of American colonial intellectual thought.

Conclusion

Other than the story of Anne Hutchinson, however, the simplistic monstrous birth scenario for the origin of the Jersey Devil has little supporting evidence. A review of the extant publications and doctors' records from the period show no references to such births in the Pine Barrens region. What remains is not Mother Leeds, but the colonial-era family patriarch, Daniel Leeds.[39]

Finally, in 1701, the Crown decided to unify the two Jerseys into a single colony. The first royal governor of New Jersey, Edward Hyde, Lord Cornbury (1661–1723), simultaneously served as governor of New York through 1708. Cornbury is remembered as one of the most vilified and hated governors in colonial America. He was accused of being a spendthrift, of being biased in his judgments, and of being prejudiced toward the Quakers. There were other allegations as well. A portrait widely believed to be Cornbury hangs in the New York Historical Society and shows him dressed as his cousin Queen Anne. He was accused of being a cross-dresser. In her reappraisal of his gubernatorial career, however, Patricia Bonomi argues that there is little but slander and innuendo concerning Cornbury's cross-dressing and some evidence that, far from being a rapacious cad, he performed his duties well. She points out that evidence of this behavior comes from a series of letters written by opponents of his who made the accusations of his wearing women's clothes between 1707 and 1709. As Cornbury was genuinely disliked, the accusations propagated. Bonomi also suggests that the infamous portrait of him in drag has no direct connection to him, the association being apocryphal.[40] Regardless of whether Cornbury was a fiscal scoundrel—he eventually left America in disgrace and financial ruin—or a transvestite, his connection to the Jersey Devil story is tangential, but important because of his association with one of the story's main protagonists.

The Devil and Daniel Leeds

W HEN LORD CORNBURY received his orders to take charge of New Jersey, the document included a list of his local councilors, which included Daniel Leeds.[1] Though "Mother Leeds" is most associated with the Jersey Devil, she herself never existed. Various members of the actual Leeds family of the eighteenth and nineteenth centuries have been vaguely attached to the legend. However, Daniel Leeds (1652–1720) occupies center stage. Had there been no Daniel Leeds there never would have been a Leeds Devil, and without the Leeds Devil there would have been no Jersey Devil. The life and work of Daniel Leeds must be understood, however, within the context of colonial New Jersey and the political and religious forces that shaped the region and time.[2]

The Early Years in England

Daniel Leeds was likely born at Leeds, England, in November 1652.[3] According to his own recollections, he was a precociously religious child. He stuttered, but did not overcome that condition until adulthood, when, in 1697, he experienced a "sudden and miraculous recovery."[4] In a poem he included in his almanac for 1712 he suggested descent from "a gentleman of Leeds in Kent." He added that his "father did a poor mechanic liv."[5] The family included brothers William and Thomas. His mother, Mary Cartwright Leeds, had her sons pray with her daily, a ritual Daniel remembered fondly. His parents were Anglicans, but they found the denomination lifeless. In 1658, when he was seven years old, they discovered the Society of Friends. It had been only two years since the early Friends minister James Nayler was arrested, tortured, and imprisoned after his intentionally provocative nude entry into the city of Bristol and the uproar it caused. Despite the dangers, Thomas and Mary Leeds took up Quakerism with enthusiasm. They did not insist that their children convert with them. The Quakers believed the individual must be drawn to his or her faith rather than pushed to it. As a result of this change of denomination, however, the intense mother and son prayer sessions ended, and Daniel felt a great loss, which caused his interest in organized religion to fade for a time.

Dissenter groups like the Quakers, also called nonconformists, came in different forms and had diverse ideas about religion, culture, and politics, which separated them from each other as well as from mainstream Anglicanism. In turn, the Anglican Church eyed them all with suspicion. The best known of these groups in colonial America, the Puritans, were joined by Ranters, Muggletonians, and others, as well as Quakers. The philosophy and teachings of the German mystic Jacob Boehme ran through some of these groups.[6] Called Behmenists by their detractors, they first appeared in England in the 1640s, and they focused on the Fall of man and the pursuit of salvation and were antiauthoritarian. Daniel Leeds was heavily influenced by the work of Boehme.

In his twelfth year, Daniel Leeds reported that "the God of heaven revived me." He experienced the first in a series of visions in which he saw "Jesus Christ coming down from heaven." It was a profound encounter, and Leeds would forever after be enamored of the centrality of unique mystical, personal experience. At the same time he questioned his worthiness for such experiences. He continued to wrestle with his inner demons and his relationship to the divine.[7] At the same time, his parents became increasingly invested in Quakerism. The Quaker Act of 1662 made it mandatory for all persons following that religion to make an oath of allegiance to the king—something the Quakers would not do—and the Conventicle Act of 1664, which made it a crime for more than five Quakers to assemble together, made their lives difficult because it prevented the Quaker meetings that were the heart of community worship. The first offense brought a fine of £5, while a second brought a fine of £10. A third offense might mean "transportation" (forced immigration) to far-off lands. In 1666, the year of the Great Fire of London, Thomas Leeds invited a group of twenty of his Quaker friends to the Leeds home in Stansted. The authorities rounded them up, and they were convicted of meeting in opposition to the law.[8]

In 1671, when he was twenty years old, Daniel Leeds had another vision, after which he found himself "afresh turned to God." This led to him to "often weeping in secret places," worried over the future of his soul.[9] Leeds began to take long solitary walks, contemplating the state of nature and the spirit in profound inner dialogues. In this he took inspiration from the writings of Jacob Boehme and also from Francis Bacon, one of the fathers of the Scientific Revolution. Bacon (1561–1626) replaced the tradition of scholasticism with a new approach based upon empiricism and inductive reasoning. This, he argued, would provide a methodology for investigating nature with the aim of producing reliable, fact-based knowledge useful for the better-

While no images of Daniel Leeds survive, this illustration—ironically of George Fox, one of his great rivals—gives a good idea of the male dress of his time.

ment of man. If Daniel Leeds could only find a way to meld the philosophies of Boehme and Bacon he might unlock deep secrets, not only about the universe, but also about the mystical relationship between man and God.

In 1672, at another meeting of Quakers, Thomas Leeds was arrested again and may have been held for a time in the Tower of London.[10] With his family hounded and his own concerns about salvation growing, Daniel had yet another, more profound mystical experience in which Jesus appeared to him. It seemed to give him a new vision of the spirit world, one that "no pen can or ought to write or tongue declare." He excitedly told some local Anglican ministers about it, but, unable to comprehend the intense personal nature of his experience, they blithely dismissed it. His parents recognized his despair and consoled his wounded piety by taking him to a Quaker Meeting and introducing him to the Society of Friends, who heartily welcomed him in. There he heard the charismatic Presbyterian-turned-Quaker Giles Barnardiston (1625–80) preach. A former soldier who had wrestled with inner demons of his own before becoming a Quaker, Barnardiston understood the emotional turmoil that Leeds felt himself drowning in. So inspired, Daniel Leeds became a Quaker.[11]

Now in his mid-twenties and refreshed in the possibilities of organized religion, Daniel Leeds married, but his new bride soon passed away. Little is known of his first wife or how he reacted to her death. With increasing social and political pressure upon the Quakers, the Leeds family made the momentous decision to travel to the New World.[12] Mary Leeds did not go with them. She died from smallpox after her husband and sons had left for America, and she never saw them again. She was buried on July 4, 1677, in the Quaker cemetery in Checker Alley, London.[13]

The Leeds men arrived in the New World sometime in 1677. Confusion exists about their crossing. American sources traditionally say they traveled on the ship *Shield*, while English sources often say the *Kent*.[14] Regardless, they arrived in Shrewsbury, New Jersey, where father Thomas settled. The Leeds sons made their way west to Burlington, where a population of enterprising Quakers had recently taken up residence. Initially Daniel worked as a cooper and then took up farming. In March, about the same time the Leeds family arrived, the inhabitants of West Jersey put together *The Concessions and Agreements of the Proprietors, Freeholders, and Inhabitants of the Province of West Jersey* (1677). Daniel Leeds signed this important document, which stressed freedom of religion, an elected assembly, no taxation without representation, and the equal rights of the Native people. For his part, Daniel set about making a place in this fledgling society at the very edges of the North American wilderness. He worked hard, developed a good reputation, and prospered.[15]

The town of Burlington had been founded shortly before the Leeds arrived. Quaker patriarch George Fox had traveled from New York across the Jerseys employing Native American guides, and he arrived at what early English settlers called the South River (eventually called the Delaware) in 1672. His visit inspired the Quakers to move to the region. The Friends who organized Burlington in March 1676 included William Penn and the future in-law of Daniel Leeds, Mahlon Stacy, who purchased the land from the local Lenape people. The Friends quickly set about building a settlement and laying out fields.[16] They considered several names—such as New Beverly and Bridlington—before they settled on Burlington. It incorporated in 1693 and again in 1733, when the Crown recognized it.

Upon disembarking from the *Shield*, the first Burlington Quakers established a Meeting, the basic Quaker religious service, but they had to meet in different members' homes as they had not yet acquired a permanent building. Leeds attended the Meeting regularly. In order to provide a central meeting place, the Friends at first cannibalized parts from the *Shield*, still anchored at the landing, to create a temporary tent-like structure. The good

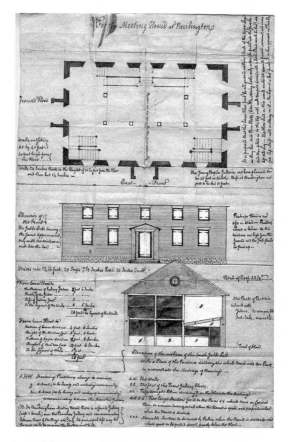

The spare but beautiful interior of the Burlington Quaker Meeting House. This is the building, which still stands, that Daniel Leeds subscribed money to help build. It was his primary place of worship until his break with the Quakers.

ship *Shield* had brought these Quakers to West Jersey, and it was held fondly by the community. As they had no plans ever to return to England, the ship no longer served the need of transportation. It would now serve them a second time, supplying ready-made lumber for the first meeting house. Parts of the *Shield* may very well have been used to build other structures and homes in the area. The tent soon outlived its usefulness, and so they began to construct a proper building. Because he wanted to build a reputation as a leading citizen, and because his piety was genuine, Daniel Leeds subscribed an initial £4 to build the first Quaker Meeting House, just off High Street.[17]

Burlington became the de facto capital of West Jersey, growing into an urban, cultural, and farming center. Initially, the town expanded slowly. Eventually, streets were laid out and soon boasted many solid brick homes and attendant paved roads, where once there had been only dirt tracks with ruts the pigs loved to wallow in.[18] A steady stream of settlers followed those first families. The town grew quickly enough that by the 1680s there were already so many drinking establishments, called Ordinaries, that guidelines to govern their operation were enacted.

Many of these early residents—including Mahlon Stacy—enthusiastically wrote back to England about the good life they had found in West Jersey. These letters attracted more settlers. The people of Burlington saw themselves as partaking in an important project. William Penn and the other Quaker leaders wanted to turn the wilderness along the Delaware River into a center of freedom and righteousness. When Philadelphia began to grow just down river, the same sensibility took hold there as well. In opposition to the exclusivity of Puritan New England, Penn saw the Delaware Valley as a place where members of any faith could congregate in peace. Despite this liberal attitude, Quakers came to dominate the political, cultural, and religious life of the area, and they did not like being challenged.

In 1681 Daniel Leeds made another attempt at marriage. Unfortunately, his new wife, Ann Stacy, died in Burlington on December 3 while giving birth to a daughter, also named Ann, who did not survive long after.[19] Daniel married a third time, to Dorothy Young, who produced eight children by 1699 and then died. He was married a final time, to Jane Revel, the sister of friend and political confidant Thomas Revel. Some variants on the Jersey Devil story name the "mother" of the Jersey Devil as "Jane," though it is unclear if Jane Leeds had any children.[20] There are no extant contemporary sources referring to any of Daniel's wives as "Mother Leeds."

In 1682 Daniel Leeds became a member of the local assembly (he also served as justice of the peace between 1692 and 1698).[21] In the many official judicial records Leeds appears in, for buying and selling land, he at first appears as "cooper." After a relatively short time he appears as "gentleman." His status rose quickly and smoothly. As he prospered from his business dealings, Daniel Leeds bought up parcels of land all over the region. He settled in a house near Jackson (also sometimes called Springfield), a hamlet just outside of Burlington, to take up the life of a successful man of local social influence. He lived most of his life in this house nestled along the banks of the Assiscunk Creek: a stream that dumps into the Delaware River a thousand or so yards away from where the *Shield* had been tied up. Leeds became part of a circle of movers and shakers, including Mahlon Stacy,

Thomas Budd (his next-door neighbor), and Thomas Revel, all of whom served on councils, surveyed land, were looked to for advice, and dreamt big dreams.

Leeds also strengthened his position by acquiring the title of surveyor general. This job carried influence: landownership disputes and boundary issues between settlers often arose in the wilds of West Jersey. It also proved a source of revenue. He laid out a number of boundaries that still exist in the twenty-first century. He used his position to acquire choice pieces of land for himself, and his name appears on many of the land purchase deeds of the era.[22]

Leeds eventually purchased land well east of Burlington near the ocean, but the town, with its proximity to the growing settlement at Philadelphia just down the river, remained a large part of his life. He surveyed Egg Harbor (present Tuckerton) on the coast as early as 1693 and may have had a residence of some kind there by 1698. When he built the first substantial dwelling in Egg Harbor, he set it upon land that "was one of the most beautiful [areas] on the New Jersey shore," as well as the most elevated point from the Highlands of New Jersey south to the cape of Virginia. He used the latest in surveying technology, including surveyor's chains, which were specially designed chains of fixed length that, when laid out, gave accurate measurements.[23] This land stood between the Great Bay to the north and Little Bay and Reeds Bay to the south on the Atlantic coast. He gave the property to his eldest son, Japhet, as a family seat. Japhet in later years made the house available as a Quaker meeting house. The location came to be known as Leeds Point: the area most associated with the modern Jersey Devil legend.[24]

Now in his early thirties, Daniel Leeds led a practical life, filled with barrel making, farming, surveying, and political maneuvering. These activities made him financially prosperous and socially important, but they did not settle his soul. His passion came in more esoteric forms. His religious philosophy, more subtle and nuanced than that of his Quaker neighbors, made his mind open to novel ways of thinking about God. He believed that one could take an active, intellectual role in attaining a connection to the Divine. Science, astrology, and mathematics gave the believer a better understanding of the mechanics of the universe and thus a better understanding of God's working in it. Scripture alone was not enough. Daniel Leeds wanted to bring the ideas of the Scientific Revolution to his neighbors as a way to facilitate godliness. Rather than sit quietly in his private study working out his cosmology, Leeds wanted others to read and understand his ideas. He had a special connection to the universe, and he wanted to share it. This became the root of his quarrels with Quakerism and would set him down a path of nonconformity even amongst nonconformists. It eventually led to the Jersey Devil.

The *Leeds Almanac*

Like many aspiring intellectuals and seekers of metaphysical truths, Daniel Leeds felt compelled to commit his ideas to paper. Taking to his pen also served as a way to circumvent his stuttering. His extensive reading of science, theology, and the occult led him to a complex belief in the efficacy of astrology. He saw the movement of the heavens as an integral part of the human experience, crucial to understanding how the universe worked. To this end, in 1686 he began the astronomical calculations needed to construct an almanac. An almanac could accomplish a number of things for Leeds. It would spread his name and influence, it would be useful to his neighbors, and it would help him contribute to the intellectual growth of his community. After much work, and with great pride, he released it the next year. If he thought his almanac would inspire his fellows, he was sorely disappointed.

The *Leeds Almanac* was the first almanac published in New Jersey. Several almanacs of varying success had been published in Boston in the preceding years, and another author attempted one in Pennsylvania. The authors of these tracts were mostly from the ranks of Harvard College graduates. Leeds, however, had received his formative education in England. As it was in England, astrology was a vital part of American almanac publishing because weather played such a vital role in people's lives.[25] The movements of the heavens had long been known to influence agriculture, and such movements could be accurately predicted. The calculations of planetary and astral movements showed sunrise and sunset, when the seasons began and ended, and what sort of weather one might expect. The Harvard almanacs also included musings on the new heliocentric astronomy. In the agrarian culture of West Jersey and Eastern Pennsylvania, where a printing industry had yet to develop, almanacs produced in New York and Boston proved useful, entertaining, and popular—but not at first.[26]

Printing had a rocky beginning in New Jersey.[27] The first permanent press did not appear until 1754, when James Parker (1715–70) set one up in Woodbridge. Parker went on to publish numerous pamphlets and government materials, including a journal called *The Reflector*, by the future first post-revolution governor of the state, William Livingston.[28] Few in power in the middle of the seventeenth century wanted printing to be practiced in New Jersey, or anywhere in the colonies for that matter. Printing could spread dangerous ideas and foment unrest, as it had in England and Europe. William Berkeley, the governor of Virginia, said he hoped no press would appear "in a hundred years." When Lord Cornbury took charge he had instructions from Queen Anne that no printing should be allowed.[29] However, few New World colonists or government officials followed any of the anti-printing edicts. Still, anyone seeking to have something printed in New Jersey would have had to go outside the region.

Luckily for Leeds, English printer and fellow Quaker William Bradford (1663–1752) arrived in the New World in 1685. Apprenticed in England to the Quaker printer Andrew Sowle and a confidant of Quaker founder George Fox, Bradford and his press came to Burlington not long after Daniel Leeds. Although Bradford became one of the foremost printers in the colonies, he is most often associated with Philadelphia (and later New York). Just where he set up his first press is unclear. In his book on the history of printing in America, Isaiah Thomas (1749–1831)—himself a printer of note and founder of the American Antiquarian Society—said that Bradford "might have, however, set up his press in Burlington."[30]

Upon arriving in West Jersey, Bradford went to work. His first project may have been contributing galleys to *Good Order Established in Pennsylvania and New Jersey* (1685), by Daniel Leeds's neighbor and friend Thomas Budd.[31] In this travelogue extolling the virtues of the region, Budd went on at length about the land, plants, and animals. This book, while initially intended for printing in America, had to be sent back to London to be finished. In 1686 a Pennsylvania man named Samuel Atkins approached Bradford about printing an almanac, a project both men saw as both useful and innocent. Titled *Kalendarium Pennsylvaniense*, it came under the scrutiny of local Quaker elders. Both compiler and printer found themselves unexpectedly on the receiving end of Church censure.[32] The local Quaker meeting warned an astonished Bradford about printing works not sanctioned by them—and almanacs were most certainly not sanctioned. Bradford ignored the reprimand, but the Atkins almanac did not go beyond this first printing.

Having been scolded by the Quaker elders for his first almanac printing project, William Bradford may have had pause to try again. When Daniel Leeds walked through the door of his print shop with his own idea for an almanac, Bradford knew what the consequences could be, but he agreed to take the project on. Going against the elders a second time could result in the ruination of his career. Despite his previous run-in, or perhaps because of it, Bradford enthusiastically took the job to print the *Leeds Almanac*. He also handed over to Leeds all of the astrological calculations—particularly the working out of the longitude of Philadelphia—that Atkins had done.

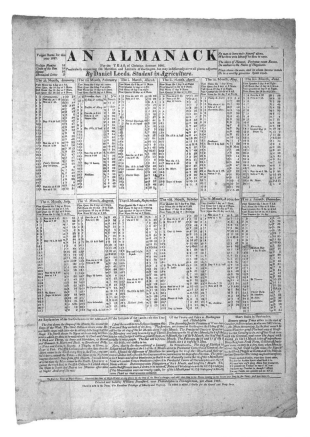

The first almanac produced by Daniel Leeds and printed by William Bradford. This is the project that began the break between Leeds and the Quakers and started the process of the creation, two centuries later, of the Jersey Devil.

With a skilled printer at his disposal and a head full of ideas, Daniel Leeds embarked on a new career as an almanac publisher and author. He and Bradford became friends. Leeds referred to himself humbly in his new publication, originally titled simply *An Almanack* and appearing in 1687, as a "student in agriculture." While the standard booklet format for almanacs had long been established in England, Bradford and Leeds initially went with a single-page broadside, which proved easier and less expensive to produce.[33] Leeds included tidal information for Philadelphia, the setting and rising of the sun and moon, and the movements of other heavenly bodies. This style Leeds took directly from the almanacs he knew at home in England. As early as 1621 British almanacs had acquired the basic layout Leeds copied,

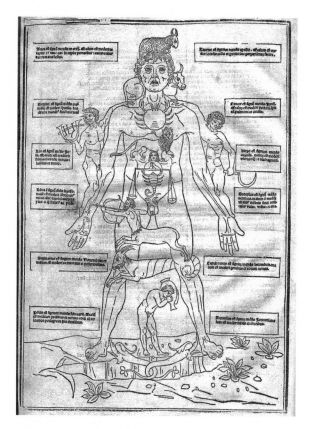

The Zodiac Man was a common feature on the covers of many almanacs, showing what was believed to be the corresponding zodiac signs that reigned over parts of the body and different ailments. It can be found in numerous variations into the twentieth century.

with masthead, astrological symbols for the months, as well as inspirational words.[34] Leeds included his own jaunty texts, such as "No man is born unto himself alone ... who lives unto himself lives alone."[35]

The agricultural, seemingly innocuous, astrological data Leeds used did not please all his readers. Not long after the almanac's appearance, several members of the Quaker Burlington Monthly Meeting complained that he used inappropriate language, as well as astrological symbols for names of days and months that were a little too "pagan" for their tastes. Leeds made connections between star signs and various human body parts—Aries for the head and face, for example—a technique common to almanacs. He used Greco-Roman "heathen Gods" names for planets.[36] In later editions he included astrological medical advice as well. "It is generally approved to be good to purge and bleed in the months of March and April," he wrote. As to bleeding, that should be done "when the moon is in Cancer."[37]

The Quakers reacted even more strongly to the *Leeds Almanac* than they had to the Atkins almanac. Civic leaders sent out an order to collect up all the copies of the Leeds almanac not in circulation and destroy them. They collected money from several elders to pay Bradford for the loss of income and assumed the incident was closed. However, Quaker doctrine held that any Friend who "so bringeth scandal upon ye truth" had to explain and apologize in order to stay in the community's good graces. In addition, "some may be ordered to go & exhort them to bring in their answers" if they failed to show up.[38] Because his almanac had supposedly offended church elders, Leeds was asked to stand up in public and address the issue. At the next Quaker Meeting he stuttered his way through an apology for having given offense, saying he did not want to do anything in "case of letting in anything against ye good practices of ye Church of Christ in Men and Women's Meetings."[39] Coming out of the Burlington Meeting House, a house he had helped build, Daniel Leeds felt embarrassed and humiliated and no longer welcome. Standing on the brick pavement of High Street, his plans thwarted for the moment, he couldn't just stop. It was a deeply emotional rejection by a community he thought of as his family. As Daniel Leeds strode down the street back home, he decided upon a new strategy.

Hurt by this rejection in the same way he had been hurt by the pastors in England who dismissed his ecstatic visions, Leeds privately had no intention of canceling his creative or philosophical work. He put aside the almanac temporarily to concentrate on his next project. This would be his magnum opus. He intended to bring the philosophy of the Scientific Revolution to New Jersey, a move he thought would enlighten and advance the intellects of his neighbors in this new community at the edge of the world. It only perplexed and troubled the Society of Friends even more, and pushed them all into conflict.

The Temple of Wisdom

Since arriving in New Jersey Daniel Leeds had spent the long, cold, snowy West Jersey evenings in his house next to the fireplace contemplating the state of man and his relationship to the universe. By now, the house was filled with the exuberant turmoil of several young children—a noise he did not mind in the least. He read voraciously in many subjects and created a file of all his favorites. This habit of collecting the written works of others as inspirations was known as "common placing" and was done by many, including the philosopher John Locke, the poets John Milton and Ben Jonson, as well as one of Daniel Leeds's heroes, Francis Bacon. Any bits of news or texts that struck the individual's fancy as useful would be copied down, or even torn out of the original and placed in a private scrapbook. Sometimes the common placer would add his own commentaries on the material. Leeds brought his common placing together with his musings to create his first full-length and most philosophical book. The year after he published the almanac, Leeds finished a manuscript he called *The Temple of Wisdom for the Little World* (1688).

The Temple of Wisdom, also printed by William Bradford, is as unconventional and ambitious a book as a colonial Quaker was likely to produce.[40] It is the first book published in New Jersey by a New Jersey author and only the second south of Massachusetts. It marked Daniel Leeds's attempt to bring the vision of science, philosophy, and theology he had learned as a dissenter's son to the New World.[41] Reading history, he declared, "makes men wise," so he filled his work with history.[42] Being essentially a published common-place book, Leeds paraphrased and copied large sections of other authors to express his personal cosmology, though he did give them credit. He included sections on angels, natural magic, astrology, theology, philosophy, and the behavior of devils. Leeds began by stating that he was no perfect writer or philosopher. "Oh no," he said, "I am as subject to be obscured by the clouds of sin and error as other men."[43] As in his almanac, Leeds included astrological symbolism. He connected the stars with aspects of God. By looking at the stars and charting their movements, "then we behold His eternal wisdom and power." The planets signify the spirits of God. Leeds made reference to the "forms and properties of nature." He told his readers that "the whole [human] body to the neck signifieth the round circle or sphere of the stars."[44]

Leeds drew upon two primary sources for his text. The first was Francis Bacon, the British philosopher and one of the founding intellectuals of the Scientific Revolution, whose work Leeds had been reading for years. As a man who had not had the privilege of attending a formal university, Leeds knew and understood the value of self-education. It irked him to see so many of his neighbors wasting their time on idle pursuits. "If a man's wit be wandering," Leeds says through Bacon, "let him study mathematic." Leeds carefully chose various essays by Bacon, including *On Deformity*, written between 1612 and 1625. This essay appealed to Leeds because of his own stuttering issues and Bacon's sympathy with the "deformed," as stutterers were often labeled. Bacon said, "Deformed persons are extreme bold." Their deformity "stirreth them to industry."[45] After years of being taunted for his speech impediment, Leeds may have found it comforting that such a person as Francis Bacon considered "the deformed" superior beings to be admired rather than monsters to be ridiculed.

The other major influence on Leeds came from the work of Jacob Boehme (1575–1624), the German Pietist he and his family had studied in England. From a humble background, Boehme had taught himself to be a philosophical theologian, claiming to have had ecstatic visions of the mystical aspect of the universe. He did not at first attempt to publish his work himself. Others copied, and passed his ideas around. Some took these manuscripts and used them to produce printed versions without consulting Boehme. The first collection of manuscripts printed behind his back came to be known as *The Aurora* (1612). It was immediately considered heretical, and Boehme had to explain himself before the local religious authorities. He argued that the fall of man was essential for his gaining entry into heaven. He saw a correspondence between zodiac signs and such human conditions as love and sweetness, or natural conditions such as dryness and sound. He created a quirky mix of theology and natural philosophy.[46] He managed to talk his way out of trouble before the magistrates, arguing that he was not a radical, but a loyal Lutheran. Having an interest in medicine as well as theology, in 1621 Boehme published *De Signatura Rerum*, in which he propounded the doctrine of signatures. This is the idea that God made many herbs, vegetables, and nuts in the shape of human body parts to help humankind understand their healing powers. Daniel Leeds saw Boehme as a kindred soul. A spiritual man like himself, Boehme had also experienced ecstatic visions and been called before religious authorities for his work.

Boehme's philosophy appealed to women like Daniel's mother, Mary Leeds, because he promoted the centrality of women in religion and the feminine aspect of God.[47] In remembrance of his mother, Leeds took Boehme's screed against the establishment and used it as the opening section of *The Temple of Wisdom* in order to speak directly to those Quakers who rejected his almanac: those "Doctors and Schollers" (Quaker elders) who had disapproved. Defending himself and his astrological work using Boehme's words, Leeds notes, "Everyone that will speak or teach of divine mysteries, that we have the spirit of God."[48]

Leeds may also have been inspired by another work with a similar title. In 1664 the philosopher John Heydon published *Theomagia; or, the Temple of Wisdome*. The author referred to himself as a "steward of God and secretary of Nature." A how-to book of practical magic, in it Heydon argued that in the distant past man knew many wondrous things, including techniques for manipulating the natural world. That wisdom had been lost to most, except a group of Rosicrucian adepts. This knowledge could be acquired once again through the use of basic astrological and alchemical techniques that Heydon listed and illustrated, with "practical interpretations and rare experiments." The *Theomagia* is an interesting book, mixing Christianity (God, angels, devils, etc.) with classical pagan notions of a goddess of wisdom and Mercury, as the inventor of grammar and music; dream interpretation; and a healthy dose of medical astrology of a kind that Daniel Leeds admired. The occult could be used, Heydon argued, as a way of finding a closer kinship with God. He did, however, accept the efficacy of magical practice far more than Leeds ever could, and Leeds never referred specifically to Rosicrucians in his texts.[49]

Like his early life in general, the details of the education of Daniel Leeds are murky, but intriguing. Leeds was largely an autodidact.[50] Literate, even sophisticated, he had a detailed knowledge of mystical theology, science, philosophy, and history. Along with the work of Boehme and Bacon (he claimed that he had "many years acquaintance with his [Boehme's] writings"), Leeds knew the writings of Galileo and Copernicus, as well as alchemists and astrologers. He does not seem to have known Latin or Greek, but English translations of these works were available to him. His name does not appear in the records of Oxford or Cambridge. As a child of dissenters, his access to those institutions would have been cut off, so the family would have had to school him at home or through the use of tutors. He also makes reference to his near contemporary, the medical astrologer Nicholas Culpepper, as well as the Roman physician Galen and the late Renaissance alchemist Paracelsus. By the time Leeds acquired his education, the philosophy of the Scientific Revolution had become part of the English education system, and many important texts had been translated into English. Jacob Boehme's *De Signatura Rerum*, which was published in English as *The Signature of All Things* (1621), proved popular and was widely read. Like Leeds, many early settlers came to America with existing educations to draw upon. Historian David Murray argues that these migrants "were not the ignorant or thriftless overflow of congested cities who sought new homes in the New Worlds."[51] They, like Daniel Leeds, who had just turned twenty-five years old when he came to America, were young, energetic, and well read. Leeds argued that science and knowledge were to be studied and used. Science, or natural philosophy, as it was then known, needed to be tempered by character, however. "Neither is it great learning," he said, "but good will that joyns men to God." Leeds reminded his readers that, in their quest for knowledge of the divine, they should be discerning and choose authorities carefully and not be taken in by works of the "fallacious astrologer," the "lying historian," the "tyrannical prince," the "murderous physician," or the "wicked magician."[52]

Taken in the aggregate, the published work of Daniel Leeds shows him to be simultaneously a Christian occultist and a purveyor of the Scientific Revolution. No "wicked magician," he rather saw himself as a pious shepherd leading his flock to the light. The meaning of *occult* has changed over time and can be difficult to pin down. In the time of Daniel Leeds, during the Enlightenment, it loosely meant a kind of hidden knowledge associated with higher ethereal planes. It could be attached to theology, spirituality, philosophy, or science. To serious intellectual enthusiasts, it could be a positive force for better understanding the workings not only of the universe but of the God who created it. For these adepts, the occult was not a simplistic practice of magic but a way to manipulate the physical world; others felt that manipulation extended only to the spiritual world. The occult can broadly be defined as a body of esoteric knowledge accessible only to a select group of adepts rather than the wider uncouth rabble. To cruder intellects, it belonged to darker spheres, and even to demonic practices.[53]

There is no evidence that Daniel Leeds ever engaged in attempts to manipulate extraterrestrial or magical processes. For him and other almanac compilers, astrology was not a dubious, fringe activity, but a proper Christian technique. As historian T. J. Tomlin notes, "Almanacs and their astrological formulations complemented and even promoted Christianity across eighteenth-century British America."[54] Less-well-educated readers of Leeds's work in West Jersey or ones who had not been Behmenists or who had known, but rejected Boehme's work, would have been unfamiliar with the esoteric nature of his writings and so saw more occultist than Christian in him. Not all Christians saw astrology as theologically acceptable. However, Boehme's melding of science and the occult was not unusual for the time or unique to Leeds. Many of the leading lights of the Scientific Revolution, with its experimental philosophy—for example, Robert Boyle and Isaac Newton—did the same. Indeed, Newton, whose pioneering *Principia* appeared in print the year before *The Temple of Wisdom*, developed not only optics, mathematics, and the laws of gravity; he also secretly followed an intense course of alchemical studies for decades, and he intensively deconstructed the Bible for hidden philosophical meanings. Leeds enthusiastically embraced a similar outlook and hoped his book would bring these ideas to his neighbors so that they could follow them as well.[55]

Despite his lofty intentions Leeds found nothing but rejection. The Quaker fathers were already uncomfortable with Leeds's astrological writing from the almanac. The Quaker Philadelphia Meeting, as the Burlington Meeting had done with the almanac, immediately suppressed *The Temple of Wisdom*.[56] The Burlington Meeting exerted power and control over Quaker life in the region, and the members did not want any heretical ideas spreading in their backyards. They "demanded and obtained general conformity" of members, and Leeds seemed to be drifting from the pure faith in dangerous, even devilish ways. American Quakers rejected mystical writings such as Boehme's. Leeds had given in to pressure from the Quaker fathers on the destruction of his almanac, and now his new book was being censured as well.[57]

Leeds had at least one fan, however. A Quaker in Massachusetts enjoyed his book so much he wrote Leeds a lengthy letter. The unknown correspondent—who, like Leeds, admired the work of Jacob Boehme—pointed out that the German had been influenced by Jewish mysticism. "Having seen what thou hast lately published in print," he said, he wanted to discuss the deeper meanings of Boehme's and Leeds's texts. Boehme, he went on, had talked with "some Rabbies of ye Jews." Thus, Boehme and Leeds both had been informed by the mystical tradition of Cabbala. He hoped that *The Temple of Wisdom* would reach a wider audience.[58] This would not be the case.

The Quakers of West Jersey had all but obliterated any trace of *The Temple of Wisdom*. It was an unusually lengthy book for the time and place, and William Bradford had printed relatively few copies before the controversy began. As a result they could be easily rounded up and destroyed. Indeed, Daniel Leeds's magnum opus, his heartfelt and deeply personal cosmology, exists today in only one known surviving copy.[59] The same thing occurred in England. Copies of his work sent to the mother country for sale were made to disappear. Other controversial Quaker authors met the same fate. The popular London newspaper *Athenian Mercury* reported in 1694 that "a great quantity of these [what they considered anti-Quaker] books being lately come over in order to sale, the chief Quakers in London bought them all up." They did this, the *Mercury* said, "designing to stifle them."[60]

Leeds once again ignored the Meeting's recommendations and determined to carry on. He had dreamed of being a philosopher wandering among the Pine Barrens engaging a metaphysical life of the mind, but the Quaker fathers ensured that his dream was dead. Rather than be a wise owl, a writer of mystical sojourning, examining the nature of the universe, Daniel Leeds would remodel himself into a rude political attack dog and do everything he could to make his enemies' lives miserable.

The Almanac Returns and the Pamphlet Wars Begin

Heartbroken over the rejection of his work, Leeds simply could not stop writing. Several years went by. He went back to square one and revived his almanac. The first issue of the reborn almanac came after the *Temple of Wis-*

dom in 1693. Leeds planned to put in everything he could, bringing his readers far more than he had in his original version. The new *Leeds Almanac* came from the press of William Bradford. Rather than using the simple broadsheet of 1687, Bradford and Leeds now chose the smaller, more traditional booklet format. This gave Leeds as many as twenty-five pages or more per issue to cover a broad range of topics. He now had a canvas upon which to display his erudition and to vent his hurt feelings, and no one was going to stop him.

As Leeds prepared to renew his almanac project, however, a new group of settlers arrived. In 1694, the area outside of Philadelphia saw the arrival of a community whose philosophical and religious leanings melded well with his. A religious group led by the German mystic Johannes Kelpius (1667–1708) took up residence near Wissahickon Creek to wait out the apocalypse. Kelpius and his followers studied the heavens looking for signs of God. They called themselves pietists—those stressing individual piety in their Christian lifestyle—a group that had originally broken from mainstream Lutheranism. Their founder was Johann Jacob Zimmerman, an astronomer and astrologer, who, like Daniel Leeds, was profoundly inspired by the work of Jacob Boehme. Kelpius took over the group when Zimmerman died, just before they left to come to America. As believers in the imminent millennium, the Wissahickon Creek mystics expected the world to end that year. Also known as the Society of the Woman in the Wilderness (a biblical reference), they referred to each other as hermits. Members lived in caves and solitary, secluded woodland spots—sometimes startling nonmembers—where they could commune with the Lord. When 1694 came and went they were devastated, yet continued to prepare for and anticipate the end of days; some disillusioned members drifted away. Upon his death, Kelpius was believed by his followers to have either discovered the legendary Philosopher's Stone of alchemical lore or to have somehow acquired it and achieved immortality.[61] Leeds must have been heartened by the appearance of this group, whose interests were so close to his own. Now he was not the only person in the region interested in astrology, alchemy, and the mystical musings of Boehme.[62]

The almanac covered all twelve months, with their inherent weather patterns, eclipses, risings and settings of the Sun and the Moon. Leeds also included medical astrology, the latest scientific astronomy, and excerpts from well-known authors; schedules of local religious meetings—ironically including Quaker meetings—court schedules, advertisements, rants on topical issues, and even highway conditions. When someone questioned his procedures for calculating the movement of the heavens, he shot back, "I oft change my method" when doing calculations. By comparison, he said, Quaker "government is greater [than I] and yet it has changed oftener here in West-Jersey than I have altered my almanac."[63]

Because Leeds wanted to raise the level of scientific literacy, he became the earliest proponent in New Jersey of the Copernican notion that the Earth orbits the Sun and not vice versa: a position not yet widely held. He accounted that the heliocentric view the "most natural to believe." He added that it is "measured by astronomers to be 195,800 miles from the Earth to the Moon." He also calculated, based upon the Earth orbiting the Sun, that "we shall find the Earth to move in an hour 5600 miles and in one minute 60 miles."[64] He told his readers to always be ready to learn new things and never "be not too forward in discovery."[65] He complained that too many of his neighbors spent their free time doing things other than improving their minds. "In too many places," he said, "the tobacco box is accounted a better companion than a library of good books." What New Jersey society needed, Leeds continued, was more knowledge of "history, law, physic [medicine], and grammar."[66] He had his own library to keep him company—a collection of some sophistication. Books on important scientific discoveries became increasingly available in English translation, and Daniel Leeds wanted his audience to read them.

First published in 1543 in Latin, Copernicus's *De Revolutionibus Orbium Coelestium* appeared in a partial translation in English in 1576. The English astronomer and mathematician Thomas Digges (1546–95) read and admired Copernicus and determined to spread word of the heliocentric view of the universe. His father, Leonard Digges (1515–59), also an astronomer, published a perpetual almanac called *A Prognostication Everlasting*. In 1576 Thomas rereleased his father's almanac, but with a special addendum containing several chapters from Copernicus in English translation. This led to an odd hybrid. Leonard Digges followed the Ptolemaic cosmology; thus the first half of the book supports the geocentric view, while the second half promotes the Copernican, heliocentric view.[67]

Following his encounters with the Catholic hierarchy over the "heresy" of supporting and promoting Copernicus, Galileo saw his work placed on the Church's "Index" of forbidden books. The heliocentric view of Copernicus and then Galileo most likely came to Daniel Leeds's attention through Thomas Salusbury and his *Mathematical Collections and Translations* (1661). Salusbury discussed and translated the essential parts of both Copernicus's and Galileo's writings into English. Leeds may have copied out by hand sections of textbooks—a common practice, as textbooks were expensive—or may have owned them himself, or possibly his father did. If so, he may have brought these texts or copies to America with him. Salusbury's work was not widely available, so Leeds may never have seen it.[68] This only complicates matters, because Leeds clearly knew and supported the heliocentric system. He must have acquired this information somewhere, but where and how eludes us. He does make reference to his own library, which would have been one of the better ones in the region. Unfortunately, no record exists of what happened to his collection.

As in the *Temple of Wisdom*, Leeds continued his practice of copying out sections of other authors' texts and adding them to his almanacs. He included parts of texts from two noted British astrologers, William Lilly (1602–81) and John Partridge (1644–1714). Lilly was a well-known and widely read astrologer who began life as a servant, but married his deceased master's wealthy widow. Financially secure, he set about teaching himself astrology and became an adept. He published several works, including *Christian Astrology* (1647), in which he argued that astrology aided rather than hindered Christians in their pursuit of the divine. Like a number of practitioners, Lilly saw astrology as a technique for gaining greater insight into proper Christianity and a deeper, more profound knowledge of God. He also published a popular almanac. Both these aspects of his life made him attractive to Daniel Leeds as a hero. Partridge appealed to Leeds for many of the same reasons Jacob Boehme did. From straitened circumstances, Partridge taught himself enough Latin, Greek, and Hebrew to enter university in Holland. He wanted to sidestep the astrologers of the Arab tradition and get back to the work of Ptolemy, whom Partridge saw as a purer practitioner of the discipline. In his Cambridge, Massachusetts, almanac for 1652, Increase Mather supported astrology, believing the stars and planets did have influence in human lives, but he denied the predictive ability of astrologers. He called William Lilly "a blind but indolent buzzard" for trying to use astrology to make specific human predictions.[69] Later, in his *Wonders of the Invisible World* (1693), Mather called astrology an "imposture."

Leeds used astrology to plot the change of seasons and the movement of the stars. He used it for the maintenance of human health as well. He followed the widely used practice of medical astrology. One of the foremost practitioners of medical astrology in England was the controversial Simon Forman (1552–1611), who tangled with the British medical establishment over licensing and qualifications and political power. Forman had thousands of clients, many of whom came from the glitterati of the day, including many members of Shakespeare's company of actors. He lived the life of a social gadfly. His celebrity came more from his behavior and his clientele than from his texts. Indeed, with one small exception, he published nothing. If Leeds knew of Forman, it was by reputation, not by reading his work. The medical astrologer and herbalist Leeds drew inspiration from was Nicholas Culpepper (1616–54). His two works, *The English Physician* (1652) and the *Complete Herbal* (1653), were widely read and appeared in numerous editions well into the nineteenth century. Culpepper argued that individuals needed to look to their own health and could do it through knowledge of medical astrology—particularly herbal remedies—and they could learn to apply these medicines for themselves.[70]

Along with Culpepper, Leeds made references to the Roman physician Galen, as well as Hippocrates and the late Renaissance alchemist Paracelsus.[71] Leeds included instructions in the almanac on where and how to harvest the herbs and flowers needed to make their own medicaments, just as Culpepper had done in *The English Physician*. Leeds explained in the 1695 almanac that the flower pennyroyal, for example, was good against drowsiness, while "Indian corn" helped with coughs. Having established himself as a purveyor of the latest science and medicine, Leeds set about establishing his other persona as critic of Quakerism.

Accustomed to criticism, Quakers were used to defending themselves in print. They made extensive use of the latest printing technology. Indeed, by the time Daniel Leeds decided to take up his pen against them, the Quakers were already old hands at defending the faith through printed works. Attackers and defenders flooded print shops—particularly in London—with hundreds of manuscripts that fairly caught fire with accusations of wrongdoing, intellectual counter-arguments, and long-winded rhetoric. When Leeds entered the Quaker pamphlet war in 1697, he found himself neck deep in a flood of works from London, Boston, and New York, praising and defending the Quakers as innocent and righteous Christians, and others condemning them as heretics.

Leeds wanted to hit back at those Quaker leaders who had censured his work and, in his mind, insulted his very soul. He placed himself in a position where he could exact his revenge. He wanted to become not just a political operative but also an author and a religious activist. To vent his resentment he combined all three. Fate turned the right way yet again for Leeds. Just as he began to contemplate his revenge against Quakerism in the early 1690s, a major schism erupted within the religion. Quarrels and doubts among members about various aspects of theology and practice went from internal discussions to outright conflicts and dissent. Leeds happily added his fuel to this fire.

The Keithian Schism

Daniel Leeds embraced the growing anti-Quaker cause in America, including backing the most notorious anti-Quaker, George Keith (1638–1716). An early member of the Society of Friends, Keith knew founder George Fox, William Penn, and the first East Jersey Quaker governor, Robert Barclay (1648–90). Keith staunchly supported the fledgling Quakers, going so far as to serve jail time on several occasions in England for his beliefs. Keith came to New Jersey in 1685, became a surveyor, and took his place as a leader within the Quaker community. He did the survey that separated East from West Jersey, and he founded the town of Freehold.[72] When Keith arrived in New Jersey he brought a considerable private library with him. He and many of his well-educated English Quaker colleagues took an intellectual approach to their faith and saw Quakerism as a text-based highbrow theology.

By 1701 Anglican leaders in London saw North America as a fertile ground for confronting the Quakers and for spreading the Church of England. To this end they formed the Society for the Propagation of the Gospels as a tool to spread Anglican thinking throughout the British colonial world. They wanted an erudite scholar to take the lead in the Middle Atlantic region, and they found their man in George Keith. Already well-established in New Jersey as a proponent of Quakerism, Keith had, much like Daniel Leeds, come to believe that the Quakers had drifted from the pure faith. Keith thought that the original Quaker emphasis upon biblical texts and the rejection of worldly goods had been abandoned. Having felt his friendly criticisms unheeded, Keith went on the offensive. He joined the Society for the Propagation of the Gospels and proceeded to use the same zeal with which he had previously supported the Quakers to denounce and attack them.[73] Daniel Leeds, too, became associated with the Society for the Propagation of the Gospels as he looked for more ways to disparage the Quakers. He also quickly learned that others in the American Quaker community had been feeling the same way.

Leeds found himself drawn to Keith in part because his preaching caused him to remember his younger days of visions and personal connection to God. Coming off his poor treatment by the Quakers, he saw Keith as another kindred spirit: a man of letters, educated, an intellectual. Taking his cue from Keith, Leeds began to search Quaker texts for problematic verses and inconsistencies, and he found plenty. Following the public rejection of both his almanac and his book, Leeds determined to leave the Friends and make a career of pointing out their shortcomings.[74]

In 1696 London Quaker apologist Caleb Pusey published *A Modest Ac-*

count from Philadelphia, a long anti-Keithian rant. Along with pointing out the apostasy of Keith, Pusey refers to "the almanac maker" who derisibly publishes "the silly idle fluff he there puts in." The "almanac maker" is Daniel Leeds. Pusey already had little respect for the *Leeds Almanac*, having declared that he "shall take a little notice of the noise he [Leeds] makes therein concerning some Quakers of Philadelphia."[75] Leeds now had a public nemesis, one with whom he would spar for decades to come. The Leeds/Pusey/Quaker book and pamphlet war had begun. Daniel Leeds would no longer allow the insults to be one-sided.

Conclusion

Daniel Leeds felt obliged to explain his position and also to defend George Keith and other Quaker controversialists. Where *The Temple of Wisdom* is a statement of personal philosophy, Leeds's next book, *The Innocent Vindicated from the Falsehoods and Slanders of Certain Certificates* (1695), stands as an outright anti-Quaker diatribe, the first of many he would write. Leeds felt some regret about contributing to "a scribbling contentious age," but said "I find it my duty to detect falsehoods and slanders."[76] In *The Innocent Vindicated* Leeds responded directly to the "slanderous writings" of John Pennington about George Keith in his *Certain Certificates*.[77] The son of adamant Quaker Isaac Pennington, John also took the defense of the Friends to heart and published a number of tracts supporting them. Along with the theology of Quakerism, Leeds attacked Quaker leaders whom he found to be full of "dis-harmony, clashes and contradictions," just like their texts. In his youth he had taken up the Quaker cause and become a Friend out of deep-seated conviction and with the zeal of a convert. His enthusiasm made the sting of rejection that much more painful and inspired him to hit back even harder.

In 1697 Daniel Leeds suddenly overcame his stuttering. Though he does not give much detail about how he accomplished this, he viewed it as an almost miraculous event. At the same time, he found his voice as a critic. His next project, *The Trumpet Sounded Out of the Wilderness of America* (1697), continued the deconstruction of Quakerism. Having defended George Keith, Leeds could now focus his wrath. Arguing that Quaker theology denied the divinity of Jesus, he accused Quakers of being antimonarchists. He left the Quakers because, he said, "they formerly exclaimed against the government of England."[78]

His apostasy is an indication of how traumatic it had been for him when his great project—*The Temple of Wisdom*—was deprecated. Leeds knew he would be attacked in turn, so he hesitated publishing the material in *The Trumpet Sounded* for "being not insensible what suffering I hereby outwardly will incur." Once his mind and heart had cleared, he saw what he had to do, because the "peaceful conscience" he acquired due to his speaking out he "esteem[ed] above all."[79] He challenged the Quakers to a public debate on the subject, but did not expect one. "But I must tell you plainly," he said to his Quaker loyalist readers, "I know you so well that I expect no such fair dealings at your hands."[80] As a result of his publication Leeds said "some of my former friends . . . have a watchful eye upon me."[81] In that he was correct; the Burlington Meeting of the Friends had grown increasingly upset with what Leeds published. In 1698 the members referred to him as "evil" for his publications and other unseemly behavior.[82] It would not be the last time Daniel Leeds or the Leeds family would be accused of demonic activity.

CHAPTER THREE

The Devil and the Founding Father

D ANIEL LEEDS had become a pillar of Burlington society, but from the moment he published his almanac, he found himself both at odds with the Quaker hierarchy and unwittingly on the road to being recast as the father of a monster. His quirky cosmology, influenced by astrology, German Pietism, the Scientific Revolution, and his own approach to the divine, ran him afoul of his West Jersey neighbors. Despite this, much of the original conflict stemmed from the censure of his almanac and *The Temple of Wisdom*. Hoping his writings would be embraced by the Friends, his feelings were hurt when they rejected them. It is unlikely he would have engaged in such a vociferous and sustained war of words with the Quakers had they taken a kinder attitude to his early works. His neighbors were outraged by his later anti-Quaker writings and his blatant rejection of their authority. They would call him a minion of Lucifer.

Had the controversy surrounding the Leeds family ended with Daniel Leeds, the Jersey Devil might never have been born. While his son Titan's works did not directly address the nature of religion and politics, his quarrels would be just as public. The publishing career of Titan Leeds thus represents the next phase of the Jersey Devil story. His encounter with Benjamin Franklin would not only mark the end of the Leeds almanac but would help sow the seeds of the legend of a monster.

The Schism Continues

In addition to riling his neighbors with his uncomfortable theological arguments, Daniel Leeds accused Quaker founder George Fox of the more prosaic crime of plagiarism and ghost writing, particularly with his *Battle Door to the Doctors of Scholars* (1660).[1] Leeds insisted that Fox had employed "certain Jews" to write it for him.[2] Leeds himself had copied out large chunks of his *Temple of Wisdom* from other books. He felt, however, that he had the moral high ground because he had openly stated in his book that he was copying. Fox, according to Leeds, was genuinely plagiarizing.

In 1699 an anonymous tract, *The Case Put and Decided*, accused Quakerism of theological wrongdoing. Its author stated that Quaker leaders such as Fox, George Whitehead, and others were dishonest, theologically confused men who used their positions and power to rig local politics—especially in the realm of land grants and purchases—to favor influential Quakers such as Edward Billing and Samuell Jennings. They put cronies into positions of power at the expense of non-Quaker West Jersey residents. They also snubbed their noses and opposed royal authority in the region.[3]

Almost immediately Samuell Jennings replied with *Truth Rescued from Forgery and Falsehood* (1699). Convinced that Daniel Leeds had written *The Case Put and Decided* but was too cowardly to put his name on it, Jennings argued gleefully as he described the book as having "stole into the world without any known author's name affixed thereto." He said this renders Leeds's work "more like its Father, who was a lyer and murtherer from the beginning."[4] For Jennings, *The Temple of Wisdom* was "father" to all of Leeds's later works, and it had attempted to kill off Quakerism.

A number of Quaker defenders rallied against Leeds. In the pamphlet war between the Quakers and their opponents, Daniel Leeds had an opposite number in Caleb Pusey. A friend of William Penn, Caleb Pusey (1650–1727) came to Pennsylvania in 1682. He opened one of the first mills in the region, entered local politics, and became a member of the provincial Supreme Court and of the executive council. Initially a friend of the heretic George Keith, Pusey repudiated him when the controversy began and focused his counterattacks upon Daniel Leeds.[5]

When the Society for the Propagation of the Gospels persuaded George Keith to be their representative in West Jersey, they wanted a church as the center of Anglican activities. They purchased land in Burlington for a building to be erected known as St. Mary's. Queen Anne, Lord Cornbury's cousin, endowed the church in 1703. Along with a building, they needed a rector, and to this end they installed John Talbot (1645–1727) in 1704.[6] He had traveled with George Keith, and the two men were respected friends. Talbot held sway as rector of St. Mary's Church until 1725. Leeds contributed money to building St. Mary's and was its warden in 1706.[7] Talbot hated the Quakers as heretics, claiming that they would not do Baptism by water but by Spirit. More prosaic reasons than theological issues included his contention that the Quakers had used influence, coercion, and nepotism to take control of local politics and had treated Anglicans like himself as second-class citizens. The Quakers, Talbot said, "are worse than infidels . . . they serve no God but Mamon and their own bellies."[8] Talbot regularly preached anti-Quaker rhetoric.[9] Making the situation even pricklier, the new church and the old Quaker meeting house sat just a block or so away, in downtown Burlington.[10] In this kind of physical proximity the two groups must have been like a pair of Renaissance-era Florentine families whose towered villas stared at each other. Congregation members, supporters and opponents, would have passed each other on the street, sat near each other at public gatherings, and talked incessantly about each other at private dinner tables.

The dislike Leeds held for his former religion seemed to know no bounds. Anti-Quaker books continued to flow from his bitter pen. In 1705 he published *The Great Mystery of Fox-craft Discovered*, in which he attacked George Fox directly as a fraud. He accused Quakers of revering George Fox in the same manner that "the Turks idolize their Prophet Mahomet." Quakerism, Leeds says, carries only the "pretense of Christianity."[11] Leeds argued again that Fox did not write his own books, but paid ghostwriters. As proof he offered up letters from Fox to a correspondent whose spelling and syntax fell well below the mark. These supposed letters from Fox contained nothing particularly egregious or controversial. They stood, Leeds argued, as examples of the uneducated and crass leadership that marked Quakerism. The letters went to Lewis Morris, the influential New York landowner. Leeds acquired them from the Reverend Talbot, though Talbot never explained how he had obtained them. They were likely forgeries. The letters accusing Lord Cornbury, for whom Leeds worked as a counselor, of cross-dressing came shortly afterward and may have been in retaliation for the contentious Fox letters.

Lewis Morris (1671–1746) owned Morrisania, a large manor in New York. He wanted to control both New York and New Jersey and went so far as to travel to England to argue against the proprietors of New Jersey, make it a royal colony, and have himself installed as governor. The Crown went along with the idea of colonial status but gave the job to Lord Cornbury instead. Outraged, Morris became a great enemy of Cornbury and worked vehemently to have him replaced. As an Anglican, Morris distrusted the Quakers, but hated anyone, such as Talbot or Leeds, who supported Cornbury. When the Fox letters became public, linking Morris to George Fox in a scandal perpetrated by his Anglican enemies, albeit a minor one, Morris and others made the cross-dressing allegations. The politics of colonial America was bare-knuckled and no holds barred. Morris's association with the Crown and his opposition to the Quakers stood as nothing compared to his own ambition and his hatred of Cornbury. In the end Morris prevailed; in 1738, the Crown finally appointed him governor of New Jersey.[12]

Satan's Harbinger Encountered

The new spiritual leader of the Anglicans of West Jersey, John Talbot, enjoyed baiting the Quakers. His animus toward the Quakers even outdistanced that of Daniel Leeds. Talbot tried to draw them into a public debate, but they would have none of it. He complained that "no they say," concerning face-to-face public debates, "they will answer in print."[13] The Friends would not have their meeting house turned into a circus, with detractors and enemies shouting at them.[14] Their dignity and their place of worship would not be sullied. Following *The Mystery of Fox-Craft*, Caleb Pusey quickly put out *Some Brief Observations Made on Daniel Leeds His Book: Entitled the Second Part of the Mystery of Fox-Craft* (1706). Pusey lamented that people not familiar with the facts believed Daniel Leeds when he disparaged Quakerism and George Fox. He did this, Pusey said, by misquoting and cherry-picking phrases and ideas and taking them out of context for a skewed political end.

It went back and forth like this for years, a tennis match in which either player swatted the opposite's serves. Accusation followed accusation, with neither side really gaining the upper hand. In *A Challenge to Caleb Pusey* (1700), for example, Leeds said his opposite number had changed "the substance of the subject to make me speak what I never intended." This, Leeds said, is designed to "render me odious."[15] Pusey then accused Leeds of doing the same to him. In *The Bomb Search'd and Found* (1705), Pusey shows in excruciating detail the "thunderous abuses" Leeds heaps upon him, "to say nothing of the miscitations [sic], clipping of sentences, and perversity of our friends writings."[16] Both sides claimed the other had been taking things out of context and misquoting. For all its prosperity and cosmopolitan affect, Burlington was still a small town. Insulting each other in print must have made for interesting face-to-face moments. Daniel Leeds soon found himself the most hated man in Burlington.

One of Pusey's most pointed and personal attacks upon Leeds appeared as *Satan's Harbinger Encountered . . . Being Something by Way of Answer to Daniel Leeds* (1700).[17] Pusey let loose with a tirade against Leeds, who then shot back to "check his lyes and forgeries" in *A Challenge to Caleb Pusey* (1700). Pusey accused Leeds of a whole range of inappropriate behavior, mostly spreading lies and "calumnies" that bit painfully at the heart of Quakerism. He did it, Pusey argued, with the venom of a demon. Leeds had, Pusey said, "galled" the Quakers with his *Trumpet Out of the Wilderness*. Leeds chuckled condescendingly, saying Pusey has so little evidence to refute his claims that he has to use George Keith's words to undermine the assertions Leeds made. "Alas poor man!" Leeds asks, "is the Quaker's cause so drooping that he [Pusey] is forced to support it with one Quaker's book to help another?" Even better, Leeds says, this tactic "duely considered, no ways helps him neither."[18]

Continuing his attack upon the Quakers and playing off the title of an earlier work, Leeds released *News of a Strumpet Co-Habitating in the Wilderness* (1701). Here Leeds referred to the "spiritual and carnal whoredoms and adulteries of the Quakers."[19] Leeds lashed out at many members of the Quaker elite besides George Fox. He charged them with adultery, fathering children out of wedlock, cheating tradesmen, and other insidious crimes. Caleb Pusey replied with *Daniel Leeds Justly Rebuked* (1702), which Leeds countered with *The Rebuker Rebuked* (1703). Leeds worked as a one-man publishing machine and center of a war of words over the efficacy of Quakerism, putting out biting and sarcastic publications with regularity. Historian Patricia Bonomi refers to Leeds as "perhaps the best surviving example of early Middle Colony scandal mongering."[20] When Lord Cornbury relinquished the governorship to return to England in 1708, Leeds left the council, but the next year he became justice of the colony's Supreme Court, presumably sitting next to his nemesis Caleb Pusey, also a justice.[21]

Pusey publically accused Leeds of both working for and being a devil. He called Leeds "evil" and a "murtherer," and finally, "Satan's Harbinger." While no one realized it at the time, this machinery of innuendo, slander, and false accusation now slowly began to turn toward creating the Jersey Devil legend.

Devilish Slander

During this period political rivals regularly ridiculed each other by calling them devils. Depictions in religious and political tracts of Satan—many of which resemble the later popular image of the Jersey Devil—go back to the Middle Ages. The Early Modern era and the introduction of wood-block printing saw the devil rendered in humorous ways as a tactic to deflate and lampoon evil or to accuse others of being devils. One such example appeared in London in 1641 and would have been known to English Quakers. That year a pamphlet feud broke out between John Taylor and Henry Walker. Taylor, known as the "Water-Poet" because of his job as a ferryman, produced a tract satirizing preachers who had no attachment to a church congregation. These men were known as "tub preachers." In retaliation, Walker published *Taylor's Physicke has Purged the Divel*, which has a crudely drawn, but startling illustration of Taylor in his ferryboat with a winged figure defecating on his face.

The image of a creature with hooves for feet, claws for hands, leathery wings, and a pointy tail did not originate with the Jersey Devil legend, but was part of a robust tradition.[22] The cover illustration for poet and playwright Christopher Marlowe's (1564–93) *The Surprising Life and Death of Doctor John Faustus* (1624) has the title character raising Mephistopheles, who looks much like the Jersey Devil. Identifying a political rival as a monster or a devil proved a useful technique and contributed to the growing popularity of political satire.[23] An example of this is *The Life and Character of a Strange He-Monster* (1726), in which a political rival is called "the scabby offspring of a Scotch Moggy by a scratching pedlar." Out of Boston came *The Monster of Monsters* (1754), which concerned a local alcohol tax. This tax, the author notes in overblown prose, stands as "the most hideous form and terrible aspect such as one as was never seen in America."[24] Unscrupulous land grabs following the Revolution resulted in *The Deformity of a Hideous Monster Discovered in the Province of Maine* (1797).[25] Colonial and Revolutionary War era America brimmed over with devils and monsters, and political rivals regularly made accusations of many types. Scandal and backstabbing in print occurred as much during the seventeenth and eighteenth centuries as it does today, and Daniel Leeds was in the thick of it. In colonial America the term *monster* often appeared in the media, but always in a political context rather than a biological one. People feared traditional monsters, devils, and witches, but now faced the added apparitions of monarchy and theocracy.

Leeds had other accusers as well. In order to boost sales, almanac publishers entered into controversies or feuds with one another, sometimes legitimate, but often made up—not unlike the manufactured controversies of modern media. In 1705 an almanac publisher named Jacob Taylor aired an attack upon Leeds in his *Ephemeris Sideralis*. He took particular aim at Leeds, going so far as to include on the cover of the almanac "some remarks on D.L." as a way to draw in readers. He accused Leeds of fumbling his mathematical calculations and of plagiarism. In referring to Leeds's *Temple of Wisdom*, Taylor highlighted the extensive use Leeds made of the work of others, like Jacob Boehme. Taylor said that Leeds had "filched matter out of other men's works to furnish his spurious almanacs." To this Leeds replied that Taylor "crows like a cock on his own dung hill."[26]

Taylor especially disliked Leeds, allowing Leeds's other adversary, Caleb Pusey, to add his remarks to the almanac. Pusey, or C.P., as he is listed rather than by name on the cover of Taylor's pamphlet, called the publications of Leeds "the false, abusive and inartificial [sic] writings of that unparalleled plagiary and unreasonable transcriber."[27]

The source Leeds copied from, according to Pusey and Taylor, was John Gadbury's *Ephemerides of the Celestial Motions and Aspects of the Luninaries* (1680), published in London. John Gadbury (1627–1704) published almanacs that covered several years rather just one at a time.[28] Gadbury would have been an interesting author for Leeds to emulate. An Oxford-trained Catholic convert, Gadbury wanted to reform astrology and bring it in line with the New Experimental Philosophy then being promoted by the recently created Royal Society of London and its members, including Robert

Title-page illustration for Christopher Marlowe's *Doctor Faustus*, published in 1620. Note the devilish creature in the lower right-hand corner. Jersey Devil–like creatures appeared regularly in religious tracts as well as literature, in this case on the frontispiece of Christopher Marlowe's play about selling one's soul to the devil.

Boyle, Robert Hooke, and Isaac Newton. This was not unlike what Leeds himself sought to do. Gadbury had even been briefly mentored by the same William Lilly whom Leeds admired, to the point of copying out sections of his work for inclusion in his almanac. Lilly suggested Gadbury study at Oxford with medical astrologer Nicholas Fiske (1579–1659).[29] Part of Gadbury's astrological oeuvre included deciphering the meaning of comets, as Lilly had done.[30] Eventually though, Gadbury had a falling out with Lilly, and the two began sniping at each other. He saw Lilly and Leeds's other hero, John Partridge, as purveyors of the worst aspects of supernaturalism. He accused them of the same sins that Pusey and Taylor faulted Daniel Leeds for: sloppy calculations and plagiarism. Leeds learned of Gadbury through William Bradford. The printer had worked with Samuel Atkins, publishing his one and only almanac. (Atkins had also worked out the longitude for Philadelphia.) When Bradford decided to print the Leeds almanac, he may have given Leeds Atkins's manuscripts. Entangled intellectual relationships abounded.

Leeds's other nemesis, Jacob Taylor (1670–1746), emigrated from England sometime during the early to mid-1690s. A devout Quaker, he used his considerable literary skills to attack anyone he deemed an enemy of the Friends. Well educated, Taylor saw himself, and the burgeoning circle of Philadelphia literati he became part of, as bringers of classical Greek and Roman attitudes and educational and cultural sensibilities to the fledgling New World. They strove to make Philadelphia a "New Athens."[31] Daniel Leeds also strove to raise the intellectual level of the Philadelphia/Burlington region. Without the schism, Leeds and Taylor would likely have become friends, but his anti-Quaker attitudes put him opposite Taylor and made him a target for Taylor's ire. Obsessed with Leeds, Taylor asked, "what Golden stars on prosp'rous Leeds did shine! Brave Daniel then whose fare should equal thine." His annoyance at Leeds became so heavy that he even referred to him in one of his astronomical poems included in his almanac. For the month of December Taylor waxes philosophic:

But Leeds exerts a thumping wit
Above all vulgar measure
Moves nature in a Jumping fit
According to his pleasure[32]

In addition to having literary pretensions, Taylor was a gifted mathematician. Shortly after arriving in the Philadelphia area he published *The Tenebrae* (1697). A book of solar and lunar eclipses rather than a traditional almanac—which he started to produce later—it is the first book of mathematical equations published in North America and the first to use steel engravings for the artwork.[33] The feud between Leeds and Taylor lasted as long as Leeds's feud with Caleb Pusey. All these men made charges and countercharges against one another over the years. When Pusey died in 1727, his devotees said of him that "much might be said of his zeal and integrity for truth."[34]

Daniel Leeds not only put himself at odds with his Quaker neighbors, but his political maneuverings gained him enemies there as well. Leeds aligned himself with the British Crown, becoming councilor to the governor, Lord Cornbury. Under Cornbury, Leeds felt he could throw his weight around. In his role as a Tory councilor, one of Leeds's first actions advised the new governor not to swear in several Quaker members appointed to the assembly by local election. Leeds, along with his oldest and closest friend, Thomas Revel (whose sister he eventually married), persuaded Cornbury to reject three men from serving even though they had been popularly elected. Leeds and Revel had reservations about Quakers gaining too much political power in New Jersey. Cornbury agreed and refused to allow the three Quakers to take their positions. This caused the Quakers to react by demanding that Cornbury change his mind. The rest of the assembly complained to Cornbury about these "groundless accusations," but to no avail. Cornbury alienated the Assembly and its Quaker population through "arbitrary practices" by being inconsiderate, listening to false accusations against its members, and not spending much time in the colony of which he was governor.[35] They saw this maneuver as an example of an overtly anti-Quaker attitude by both the local and the distant British governments. It was not long before political pressure mounted to a point where Daniel Leeds no longer wanted to participate in the process he had so gleefully entered. He continued to publish his almanac, but in 1714 he retired from public life. He turned the business over to his sons Felix and Titan, who took charge of the publishing and compiling.[36] Ultimately, politics drove Daniel Leeds to retirement rather than to theology.

Titan Leeds

Of all the sons of Daniel Leeds, Titan most followed his father's intellectual pursuits. A natural polymath, Titan Leeds (1699–1738) early on showed aptitude in math, science, and astronomy. He had already been doing the calculations for the almanac, and he had a gift for anticipating lunar eclipses. Like his father, Titan loved sitting for hours at his desk covered with papers and books, working out the secrets of the universe. Initially, both Titan and the youngest Leeds son, Felix, ran the almanac. The lack of enthusiasm Felix felt for such an undertaking soon showed, and Titan took sole charge. Daniel beamed with pride while introducing his son to the reading public. He told his readers not to worry about Titan's age (he had only recently turned sixteen):"while he lives with me he shall not be wanting."[37] Writing and publishing the *Leeds Almanac* became Titan's primary occupation. He spent most of his life living in the original Leeds plantation outside Burlington with his father.

Just because the outspoken Daniel Leeds no longer published his screeds or engaged in political wheeling and dealing did not mean the controversy surrounding the Leeds family had died away. After taking over the almanac,

Titan found that the Leeds family still had enemies, and that devils were everywhere. Titan shared his father's zeal for science but not his father's zeal for battling with Quakers. As a result, he never published any material other than the almanac. Taking over from such a politically contentious public figure was no small job. His father was Satan's harbinger: no small accusation in colonial America. These attacks transferred to Titan, as well, and could not be easily shaken off. Walking down the streets of Burlington and other Pine Barrens towns, Titan would have encountered disgruntled Quakers and supportive Anglicans alike.

Despite his father's public battles with the Quakers and conversion to the Anglican faith, Japhet Leeds (the eldest son) used his house, built upon the land Daniel had surveyed himself and purchased for his son at Leeds Point, as a regular meeting house for the Quakers.[38] Most of Daniel's children did remain loyal Quakers, though some became Baptists and others Presbyterians. It is unclear whether Titan followed his father into apostasy or not.

In 1720, after years of first trying to uplift and inspire his neighbors and then arguing with them, Daniel Leeds quietly passed away. The great Keithian Schism had petered out, the pamphlet wars dried up, tensions settled, and life in West Jersey went on.

Titan tried to publish the almanac with as little friction as possible. Regardless, he had his share of public encounters. In 1720, the year of his beloved father's death, Titan mentioned that he might not be able to continue publishing the almanac because an unnamed monstrous rival was giving him grief. "If I write no more," he said, "you may think 'tis because of a smoak breathed out to stifle me by the Devil's emissary." This person, this Devil of Leeds, was guilty of "lying, cheating, treachery, malice, and damb'd hipocrasie." Where his father had once been labeled Satan's harbinger, now Titan Leeds used a similar title for another. It is not clear whether this "Devil's emissary" was a genuine person or simply represented the grief he felt at losing his father. Daniel had been Titan's mentor, his advisor, and the rock he leaned upon in hard times. Now Titan was on his own, and the devil never seemed far away.

Demonic influence concerned many in early America, and so any author wishing to tarnish the image of a rival could make him out to be a monster or a devil. In *The Armour of Christianity: A treatise, detecting first, the plots of the devil against our happiness* (1704), Cotton Mather argued that there are many devils afoot, and a goodly Christian must always be on guard.[39] Benjamin Keach, in *War with the Devil* (1714), likewise warned his fellows of the wiles of the evil one. It is unclear just whom Titan Leeds meant when he referred to his enemy as the Devil's emissary, but it would not be long before he fell afoul of yet another, and found himself in one of the most notorious almanac feuds of them all.

The Quakers are a central influencing factor in the creation of the Jersey Devil legend. When Daniel Leeds arrived in America in 1677, Quakerism had been in existence barely longer than he had. The Jersey Devil mythos stems in part from the Quaker relationship to the supernatural. Publically and officially, Quaker doctrine renounced witchcraft and the occult as foolishness. Privately, many Quakers enjoyed and were titillated by ghost stories and fascinated by the supposed behavior of witches. They rejected witchcraft, but did not persecute it the way the Puritans of New England did. When the infamous witch trials broke out in Massachusetts in 1692, the Quakers were not involved; indeed, the Quakers of New England barely escaped accusations themselves. Quaker founder George Fox railed against belief in the occult yet at the same time claimed he could spot a witch just by looking at her. "The Lord," he wrote, "had given me a spirit of discerning," so he regularly accosted women, telling them to repent. A story from his life would reverberate in an occult tale years later in America. While they held him imprisoned in England in 1659 as a heretic, Fox's jailers insisted on sitting in the fireplace of his room because they feared "I should escape up the chimney," a feat not unlike that supposedly performed by the Leeds Devil in 1735.[40] The Quakers always had a somewhat fluctuating attitude toward the occult. While they acknowledged such practices took place, they never really felt compelled to do much about them other than wag their fingers and tut-tut about it in public.

Benjamin Franklin

Born in Boston in 1706 just as the Daniel Leeds–Quaker feud hit its stride, Benjamin Franklin grew up to be an inventor, statesman, and illustrious American personage. Because he came from a large and somewhat impoverished family of brothers and sisters, his parents hoped he would enter the clergy. Instead, he apprenticed with his brother James as a printer. In 1723 James began to publish the *New England Courant*, thought to be the first newspaper in Boston. Yearning to write, but knowing his brother would never let him do so because of his age, Benjamin submitted letters under the female pseudonym Silence Dogood. These letters enthralled the staff with their wit and sagacity, but neither they nor James knew that the young Benjamin had written them. Then fate stepped in. Because of his public print battles with the powerful Boston clergy, particularly the Mather family, James was briefly jailed for publishing material the Mathers saw as scandalous. This allowed Benjamin to take control of the shop and its publications and keep them all running: oddly, something that James did not appreciate. When James returned, he put increasing pressure on Benjamin.

Seeking his own future out from under his brother's influence and control, Benjamin left Boston for Philadelphia. After apprenticing with a printer there he traveled to London, at the behest of the governor of Pennsylvania, to purchase printing supplies. To the governor, the young Franklin was enthusiastic, eager, and expendable. The governor, however, had not given Franklin the proper funds to buy the supplies. The scheme fell apart, and Franklin had to find work in London for several months in order to earn the money to get home. Arriving back in Philadelphia, Franklin took his savings, borrowed more, and opened a print shop of his own. He soon showed a profit. He purchased the *Pennsylvania Gazette* and made it profitable, as well. Franklin then set his sights upon the lucrative almanac-publishing market. This brought him face to face with Titan Leeds. Though he had no way of knowing it, Franklin's decision to begin competing with the Leeds family would help create the legend of the Jersey Devil.

Benjamin Franklin entered the almanac game in 1732. Having successfully created an alias in Silence Dogood, he made his almanac the work of his alter ego, "Poor Richard" Saunders. This would become the most famous almanac in American history and destroy its chief competition, the *Leeds Almanac*. Franklin took the name Richard Saunders from an English medical astrologer, mystic, and alchemist. The real Richard Saunders, a friend of well-known English astrologer William Lilly, began publishing an almanac in 1656 he called *Rider's British Merlin*. Saunders himself employed a pseudonym, calling himself "Cardanus Rider." Along with the usual almanac fodder, Saunders included material on medical astrology, chiromancy, and palmistry. Franklin simply lifted the entire concept and made it his own.[41]

Writing as Richard Saunders, Franklin followed the standard formula of agricultural and astrological material, including the inspirational quotes.[42] As a competitor in a lucrative market, he decided to go after his successful rival in print by creating an almanac feud. Rather than sound the more serious tone of the *Leeds Almanac*, Franklin went for a folksier, almost comical and satirical approach.[43] In the 1733 edition of *Poor Richard's Almanac*, Franklin, writing as Saunders, used astrological techniques to predict Titan Leeds's death on October 17 of that year. He referred to Leeds in his typical jaunty manner as "my good friend and fellow student" of astrology.[44] He explains that "he [Titan Leeds] dies by calculation made at his request, on Oct. 17, 1733.... By his own calculation he will survive till the 26th of the same month. This small difference between us we have disputed whenever we have met these nine past years; but at length he is inclinable to agree with my judgment. Which of us is most exact, a little time will now determine."[45] Franklin had ready models to follow for his jabbing at Titan Leeds. The Irish author Jonathan Swift (1667–1745) had already done something similar. In 1708 and 1709 Swift, who would become famous for *Gulliver's Travels* (1726), created a sort of alter ego in Isaac Bickerstaff. For Swift, Bickerstaff was a tool to satirize those things he found repugnant or ridiculous. One of these things was astrology—another, the Catholic Church. The popular British astrologer John Partridge had written a critical article on the supposed infallibility of the Church, which he ran in his 1708 almanac. In response, Swift had Bickerstaff claim that astrological calculations had shown that Partridge was about to die, and then he died. The hoax worked so well that followers of Partridge reacted with grief and despair. Some even planned a funeral for their favorite astrologer.

Franklin also used another false prediction originally made by the printer Thomas Fleet of an impending death of Boston postmaster Philip Musgrave in 1721. An almanac compiler, Fleet disliked the Boston postmaster. Under the pseudonym "Sidrofel," and calling himself "an old monger," Fleet claimed that Musgrave would die soon as predicted by the stars. Not only did Fleet use a false name, but he published his prophesy in James Franklin's *New England Courant* rather than in his own *Almanack of the Coelestial Motions*. Eighteenth-century media commentators had much in common with twenty-first-century media trolls. As an apprentice in his brother James's shop, young Benjamin would have been familiar with this hoax and perhaps even set the type for it. The public form of Franklin's feud with Titan Leeds was nothing new.

Benjamin Franklin employed these types of ruse upon his own publishing rival Titan Leeds. It must have given him a special sense of glee knowing that Daniel Leeds had been such an outspoken advocate of John Partridge as well as William Lilly. Franklin approached all this in a humorous vein. Titan Leeds, however, did not. By now his father was long dead, and Titan had no one to go to for advice. When he was attacked in print Daniel Leeds would go on the offensive, gleefully trading shot for shot with his enemies. Titan tried to do the same. He retaliated in the *Leeds Almanac* by saying that Franklin "has manifest himself a fool and a lyar" for his antics. Franklin replied with mock outrage, saying Leeds was "too well bred to use any man so indecently and so scurrilously" so this must not be the real Titan Leeds, but a manifestation from the spirit world.[46] He said he had "receiv'd much abuse from the ghost of Titan Leeds." When he referred to Leeds, Franklin always did so with the language of the astrologer. "The stars are seldom disappointed," he said when he predicted Leeds's death. The only reference Franklin made to Daniel Leeds came when he said that Titan followed "the honor of astrology, the art professed both by him and his father."[47] Titan could do little but fume. Even after Titan Leeds finally died, in 1738, Franklin published a faked letter from him written from the great beyond. Franklin's ghost of Titan says that he can see much further into the future because, having died, "I got free from the prison of the flesh."[48] Franklin then responded to his own creation that "Honest Titan, deceased, was raised [from the dead] and made to abuse his old friend [Franklin]."[49]

Franklin used his considerable satirical writing skills to expose religious beliefs he thought foolish, as well as superstitions and myriad misunderstandings of how the world worked. His clever statements about Leeds were, in reality, an attempt to discredit his almanac competitor by linking him to Satan. In that age it was not unusual to paint one's enemies as stargazing agents of the devil. The fact that Leeds promoted a belief in astrology in his popular almanac made perfect fodder for the clever Franklin. In fact, Franklin had penned a play, *Titian Pleidades*, in the late 1720s, clearly associating Leeds with astrology.[50]

Franklin's use of the hoax against Titan Leeds had several purposes. It afforded him an opportunity to attack the credibility of the editor of his competition for almanac sales, but he also saw a chance to discredit those who, like Leeds, promoted astrology. Franklin wanted to make all astrologers look like fools, this being a frequent theme in some of his satirical writing. Benjamin Franklin had cast his rival almanac publisher as a ghost, a reanimated sorcerer who haunted his enemies. The traditional "birth" of the Jersey Devil coincides roughly with the death of Titan Leeds, as well as with the Franklin-Leeds almanac war.

Franklin continued these false stories and hoaxes until nearly a decade after Titan's death, when he wrote "The Speech of Polly Baker." Upset with the way mothers, but not fathers, found themselves on trial for having children out of wedlock, Franklin put the fictional Polly Baker on trial, where she gave a moving speech in her defense. This trial was her fifth for such an offense. She was poor, had no help, and received no sympathy from society or the courts. For Polly, pregnancy was a crime that pushed her to the margins of society, not unlike a witch. First published in the British *Gentleman's Magazine* for that year, it was published again in the *Great Advertiser* in April. In Franklin's story, the woman was not convicted and ultimately persuaded one of the judges on the case to marry her. Many readers thought the story genuine. Franklin didn't confess to this hoax until 1778.[51] This fiction has similarities and themes that became part of the Leeds Devil legend: persecuted mother, absentee father, social shunning, and hypocrisy.

An Image Takes Shape

The popular image of the Jersey Devil has several sources. Along with pamphlet and broadside depictions of the devil that were well known to eighteenth-century readers, the coat of arms of the Leeds family also provides a possible source. In 1725, before the almanac feud with Benjamin Franklin, Titan Leeds changed the masthead of the almanac. Titan's brother Felix had run the almanac on and off in the 1720s. He may have been responsible for the initial change of masthead from the simple text version of their father's period to a bucolic reclining figure.[52] In 1728 Titan replaced the figure with the Leeds family crest, a shield with a solid belt, or fess, running horizontally across the middle (a symbol of the family's readiness to serve the public good). Above and below the fess are a trio of figures with wings, clawed feet, and a pointy tail representing valor.[53] These single-headed eagles appear often in English heraldry. Hovering over the top of the shield is a cockatrice, a kind of monster rooster well-known in myth.

The family emblem is authentic, though questions remain as to whether this particular Leeds family had the right to its employ. Families commonly appropriated family insignia. Titan only used it after Daniel's death. As with so many aspects of the early part of the Leeds family chronicles, there are no records showing if this branch was authorized to use the crest legitimately according to the British rules of heraldry.[54]

Now printed by Andrew Bradford, William Bradford's son, by 1714 the almanac also included an illustration of a human figure surrounded by astrological symbols that were oriented to the various parts of the body. Such a drawing, known as a Zodiac Man, was a common illustration in medical astrology in both manuscript and printed books, and it became a staple of almanacs.

In 1734 Titan sold the house his father had built just outside Burlington. This was Daniel's original plantation, where he had lived most of his life. In 1720 the estate was inventoried and assessed at more than £620 pounds sterling, a not inconsiderable sum.[55] The plantation consisted of 300 acres, 100 of which had been cleared for farming, along with the attendant buildings. The large stone and brick house in which the family lived had great sentimental importance to Daniel Leeds: it formed the center of his universe. It was the first home he built in America, he raised his family here, and he wrote the almanac and *The Temple of Wisdom* here. He grieved the deaths of his wives here. Sitting in front of the fireplace, he contemplated the cosmos and dreamt of living the life of a philosopher.

The Bradfords continued to publish the *Leeds Almanac* after Titan's death. Now called the *American Almanac*, they kept Titan's name on the cover (one or two other New York printers may have appropriated the Leeds name and published unofficial almanacs to capitalize on any remaining good will).[56] In the edition for 1738 Andrew Bradford introduced some anti-Catholic rhetoric into the almanac in a way Titan would never have done. He said that some believed the End Times were approaching and that God was about to judge all mankind. As a result, he said, "perhaps then will be the beginning of the pouring forth of the seven vials, or the last plagues upon Babylon or Tyrius, ie, the Papacy." By the later 1740s even the Bradfords gave up on publishing the almanac, and it too finally died. The family then receded from the public eye.

The Leeds family's unintentional inspiration for the Leeds Devil springs from how their reputations—both real and manufactured—were remembered in their community. The elements of the Jersey Devil story percolated and fermented over the next century. The leisurely pace of this transmutative process meant that not until the late nineteenth and particularly the early twentieth century did the legend fully arrive.

Conclusion

With the deaths of Daniel Leeds and then his son Titan, the Leeds family slipped from the public eye. They did not, however, disappear. The family continued to grow and prosper throughout the region. Jeremiah, Japhet's grandson and Daniel's great-grandson, was born and raised in the Leeds Point house. His name, too, has occasionally been associated with the Jersey Devil. Shortly after the Revolutionary War began, he enlisted in the local militia. He served under several different captains as a private. While serving with Captain Zephaniah Steelman he saw action at Haddonfield against a detachment of Hessian mercenaries in the last days of 1776. Forced to withdraw from the area, Leeds's unit moved to Bordentown, where they joined American forces leaving to meet George Washington's troops upon completion of the legendary battle at Trenton on Christmas Day, 1776. They all then engaged in the Second Battle of Trenton, when British forces counter-attacked. Following that engagement, Washington, along with Jeremiah Leeds, repaired to Princeton.[57] Jeremiah served faithfully and showed himself a leader. Later in 1777, Leeds was promoted to second lieutenant under Captain Joseph Conover.

Jeremiah's unit was then ordered to head to Red Bank to support Washington's troops, which were engaged in a battle there. They arrived on October 22, just as the shooting ended, so did not take part in that action. Despite their efforts at Red Bank and Fort Mercer, on the Delaware River, the colonials could not force the British out of Philadelphia, and the two sides separated for the winter. Jeremiah Leeds and his men then moved east back, ironically, to Leeds Point, where they took up guarding positions, there and at nearby Absecon Island. As they arrived they witnessed a British warship making its way to the open Atlantic Ocean run aground. Rather than let it be captured by the Americans, the crew set the ship on fire. With this action Leeds's ten and a half months of service in the Continental Army came to an end. Years later he would be awarded a sixty-dollar-a-year pension for his service.[58] Along with Jeremiah, a number of Leeds men served—so many that the Gloucester County infantry could have constituted its own platoon.[59]

Following his war duty, Jeremiah Leeds began purchasing land a few miles south of Leeds Point. This area is a warren of islands, bays, and inlets of varying sizes. Jeremiah had his first home in Leeds Point, on the mainland. In 1779 he began raising livestock on the offshore island, at first called Leeds Island and now called Absecon Island. He was considered the first settler of what is today called Atlantic City. His children, however, were born at his home at Leeds Point, on the mainland. Over time, he and his father-in-law purchased much of the available land on the island, which came to be known as Leeds Plantation. His first wife was Judith Steelman. His second wife, Millicent "Aunt Millie" Steelman (1792–1873), ran a tavern there long after Jeremiah's death. Their son Chalkley S. Leeds (1824–1908) became the first mayor of Atlantic City in 1854.[60]

CHAPTER FOUR

The Birth of the Jersey Devil

O N   T H E   M O R N I N G of July 4, 1788, while cruising off the Barbary
Coast, the American passenger vessel *Columbia* had a strange encounter. A geyser of water erupted alongside the ship, almost cap-
sizing it. The passengers and crew could not believe their eyes. Out of the
frothing water "a terrific monster of gigantic size" burst forth. Mermaid-like,
the creature appeared part man, part woman, with three faces, multiple eyes,
and wings. Rather than attack the ship the creature began to speak to them
in a "voice like thunder." The world was in chaos, it said. Everywhere in
Europe, Asia, and Africa, tyranny ruled. The United States as well was "now
in a state of anarchy." The monster bellowed, "You are highly favored, you
Americans." The citizens of the United States had to come together, to work
for a bright future of peace, prosperity, and economic growth. They must
"learn war no more." If they did these things, the creature said, America
would lead the world into "the foretold Millennium."[1] Having said its piece,
the creature dove back beneath the waves never to be seen again. Showing
itself on the Fourth of July could not have appealed more to patriotic Americans. Its appearance on Independence Day showed that America was special.

This patriotic apparition fit well into the tradition of monsters as portents. Indeed, the word *monster* comes from the Latin for bringer of visions
and prophesies. Monsters were by nature impressive. Such a story would
have been interpreted by American readers as support for the Revolution,
which in 1783 had just ended, although George Washington would not take
office as first president for another eight months. Monsters in America came
in various sizes and shapes, from snake-like to humanoid. Some live on in
memory; some, like this talking mermaid, fell by the wayside; others, like the
Leeds Devil, found new life on the brink of extinction.

The United States in the Nineteenth Century

The Early Republic was a time of patriotic fervor: Americans had fought a
successful revolution and, after a period of transition, established a constitution (the Barbary Coast mermaid appeared on the first Fourth of July following the ratification of the Constitution). Americans looked to a bright
future, free from the superstition and religious intolerance of the Old World.

They may have felt they had vanquished the monsters of monarchy and empire, but the American landscape would reveal monsters yet unseen.

Following the turmoil of the Revolution, settlers headed off into the interior in search of new lands and opportunities, increasingly clashing with the Native people. Immigration began to pick up again after the lull during the Revolution. US and British tensions simmered, erupting again in the War of 1812. The growing animus over slavery would eventually bring on the cataclysm of the Civil War. Moreover, the nation had a monster problem: monsters seemed to be everywhere.

A question often asked about Jersey Devil stories is, how could people be taken in so easily to believe in such an outrageously peculiar creature? The answer comes from a complex interplay of culture, economics, politics, scientific advancement, and the growing efficiency of communications. Part of that answer also lies in the now mostly forgotten precedents that had been established prior to the Jersey Devil's appearance. Throughout the nineteenth century America teemed with reports of bizarre creatures, weird happenings, supernatural events, and other incidents of the strange. America was a virtual fairyland of giants, sea serpents, devils, and spectral entities. The American interior presented itself to the Euro-American settlers as a terra incognita where anything, monsters included, might slouch and bellow. The blank spaces of the nation's imagination filled up slowly but steadily. Naturalists fanned out over the landscape collecting specimens and describing animals and the environment. The landscape of the New World and the new United States fascinated people at every level. Local natural history societies and museums sprang up as the enthusiasm for science grew. Often the most popular exhibits centered on taxidermies of exotic animals. So strange were some of them that not everyone who saw them believed such flora and fauna actually existed. When Thomas Jefferson sent a stuffed moose to Paris, for example, many there assumed it was a hoax.

The strangeness of the West bred fear of the unknown to settlers in the East. Thomas Jefferson and Benjamin Franklin both thought monstrous creatures inhabited the unexplored territories. So rampant was the belief in monsters in America that a dragon-like horse or deer born of a human mother did not pose difficulties: it didn't even really stick out. Along with the monsters created in the nation's psyche, the discovery of flesh and blood monsters provided more than enough physical evidence of their existence. They all helped pave the way for the Jersey Devil.

The idea that America contained many wondrous and strange animals and even monsters began as soon as the first Europeans arrived. Early traveler's reports are filled with breathless descriptions of flora and fauna. In his

History of the Colony of Nova Caesarea, Samuel Smith said, "the snake creeps to the foot of a tree, and by shaking his rattle, awakens the little creatures which are lodged in it; they are so frightened at the sight of their enemy, who fixes his lively piercing eyes upon one or other of them, that they have no power to get away." There is the lion, which, "by his terrible roaring in the woods, rouses the lesser beasts out of their holes."[2] Other authors told of muskrats, elk, and large and terrifying wolves.

Not all the discoveries of bizarre life came in the form of living animals. In 1705 the skeleton of a large, strange creature came to light at Claverack, New York, discovered by marl pit workers. A farmer initially found only a large odd tooth. He traded it to a local politician for a glass of rum. This politician then presented it to the governor, Lord Cornbury, who promptly sent it to England labeled "tooth of a giant." Further digging at the site uncovered large skeletal parts of what some said looked like an African elephant. Because of its strangeness, the remains came to be called *Incognitum.* Some thought the presence of such a creature in America supported the idea that the Bible was correct in saying there were giants in the earth, and that God did indeed have a special future for America mapped out. Such elephant-like remains turned up from time to time across the colonies.

In 1739 another similar skeleton was unearthed in Kentucky, and then another showed up in Newburgh, New York, in 1783. The artist Charles Willson Peale (1741–1827) immediately traveled to New York and purchased the partial skeleton and the rights to do more digging. Peale, along with being a skilled painter, was also an amateur naturalist with a fascination for the wildlife of America. He thought, too, as did the later promoters of the Leeds Devil, that monsters could be good for business. In Philadelphia he had already opened one of the first museums in the new nation, and he knew that natural history had a public appeal, especially if one could somehow make it patriotic. He had the skeleton cleaned and mounted, filling in the missing parts with papier-mâché substitutes. He then produced an impressive oil painting of the excavation of the creature with himself prominently displayed. The monstrous Mammoth, as it was now being called, drew wide popular attention and became something of a national mascot. Benjamin Franklin speculated on its eating habits, while others felt its existence proved that America produced animals to rival the rest of the world.[3]

Not all monsters walked the earth; some swam. In the 1830s bizarre and unusual skeletons began turning up along the English coast. Found in marine deposits, the fossils from the seaside town of Lyme Regis combined the characteristics of crocodiles, fish, and reptiles. Their flippers and long necks and tails put them more in line with the monstrous denizens of mythology than with any living creatures. Initially found by the amateur collector Mary Anning (1799–1847), these fossil creatures came to the attention of scientists. The naturalist Everard Home commented on Anning's discoveries, noting that they were "one of the connecting links in creation, formed for the purpose of preventing any void in the chain of imperceptible gradations, from one extreme of animated beings to another."[4] They showed, so Home claimed, that God made these creatures so that the great chain of being of all life on earth would be a smooth one, and not full of heretical, question-producing gaps. He suggested the fossil be called *Proteosaurus*.[5] In 1818 Charles König dubbed the short-necked fossil sea monsters *Ichthyosaurus*. In 1821 Henry de la Beche and William Conybeare labeled the long-necked versions *Plesiosaurus*.[6] Practitioners of the new sciences of paleontology were uncovering exciting new facts about the earth and its life. It was a heady and romantic time for science and monsters.

Because these marine reptiles were often referred to as such in books and monographs, the fanciful language of monsters and dragons joined the technical lexicon of paleontology. Plesiosaurs and other extinct marine life became popular characters in nineteenth-century depictions of the ancient world, which included exacting renderings of ancient fossil plant life. They were shown more often than not as mythical-style monsters battling in primordial seas in epic and dramatic struggles of life and death, but as real rather than imaginary beings. George Richardson, in *Geology for Beginners* (1843); Franz Unger, in *The Primitive World* (1851); Louis Figuier, in *Earth Before the Deluge* (1863); W. E. Webb, in *Buffalo Land* (1872); and many others depicted fossils in this sensational manner. Though no such marine fossil creatures came to light in North America, they did become widely known there.

As Mary Anning unearthed the aquatic fossil monsters, an entire family of land-based contemporaries came to public notice. Starting in the 1830s with the discoveries of English country doctor Gideon Mantel (1790–1852), the remains of large terrestrial reptiles of a kind never seen before swept both scientific and then popular imagination. Eventually dubbed dinosaurs, they became media darlings. Their fossils proved conclusively that they had existed and were not hoaxes. They also were not confined to the Old World.

Joining the mammoth as American monster, an even more bizarre creature turned up in 1838. That year a New Jersey farmer dug into a marl pit. Along with the thick black mud, he pulled up a collection of odd bones. They seemed so odd and strange the man brought them to his home in Haddonfield (not far from Burlington) and put them on display. Years later, in 1858, about the time that W. F. Mayer was writing the earliest known article on the Leeds Devil, lawyer and amateur fossil hunter William Parker Foulke (1816–65) took his summer vacation outside Haddonfield. There he heard the story of how nearby a monstrous set of bones had been discovered twenty years earlier. He hired some workmen and began his own excavation. He began unearthing more related skeletal (actually fossil) parts. He came up with most of a pair of large hind legs, an almost complete arm, tail vertebrae, and teeth: about 30 percent of a dinosaur. The first-ever such creature found in the Americas, it caused a sensation. Soon Joseph Leidy (1823–91), the renowned paleontologist at the University of Pennsylvania and the Philadelphia Academy of Natural Science, arrived on the scene and saw the creature for what it was.

Leidy in turn engaged the well-known British artist Benjamin Waterhouse Hawkins to do a life reconstruction of the creature. Hawkins (1807–94) had worked extensively on the reconstruction of dinosaurs in England, designing the large sculptures of the *Iguanodon*, *Megalosaur*, and other prehistoric beasts under the direction of Professor Richard Owen for the famed Crystal Palace in London. Leidy and Hawkins also produced a full-scale skeleton of the Haddonfield monster, filling in the missing parts according to the concept of comparative anatomy in the same way Charles Willson Peale had reconstructed the mammoth. The rebuilt skeleton became a popular attraction at the Philadelphia Academy of Natural History. Leidy christened the creature after the man who had found it and the place it had been found: *Hadrosaurus foulkii*. The mammoth and the hadrosaur proved that strange monstrous creatures had roamed the American northeast and New Jersey in particular.

With the discovery of fossils and monsters from antediluvian times, some people thought such creatures might still exist. The concept of extinction—proposed in the earlier part of the nineteenth century—had yet to be widely accepted. A number of naturalists thought mammoths and sea monsters might still inhabit the largely unexplored western territories. As the United States had an extensive coastline, it was only a matter of time before sea serpents would begin to appear.

The New England Sea Serpent

Along with the genuine fossil monsters, there were others of less dubious character. Sightings of sea serpents and lake monsters appear in Native American lore as well as in stories told by European explorers and settlers.[7] Sightings of mysterious sea creatures off the coast of Massachusetts go back to the 1600s. During the summer of 1817 a number of eyewitnesses claimed to have seen a serpent-like monster prowling the waters off Gloucester and

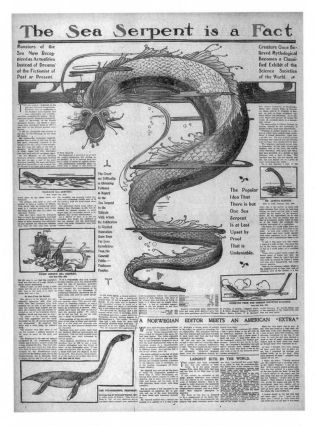

America has a long history of monster sightings, including sea serpents along the Atlantic coast.

Cape Ann, Massachusetts. The media from Boston to New York and beyond buzzed with eyewitness reports and speculations about what this creature might be.[8]

Amid the excitement, the Linnaean Society of New England believed that these stories presented an opportunity for American science. The society saw the Gloucester monster as a chance to show off its scientific acumen and generate social and intellectual respect. They mobilized their forces to solve the riddle. Correspondents sent in reports and eyewitness testimony, which the society collated for publication. They also engaged a local justice of the peace, a former Massachusetts state senator, to collect depositions from witnesses. The resulting *Report of a Committee of the Linnaean Society of New England Relative to a Large Marine Animal Supposed to be a Serpent* (1817) was made up of these eyewitness stories rather than scientific analysis. A farmer had killed a snake near the beach around the time of the sightings, and locals thought this might be a baby monster. Society representatives examined the dead creature's remains. Assuming the dead animal to be a juvenile form of the sea-going beast, the society named the Gloucester monster *Scoliophis atlanticus*. Adding to the discussion, Professor William Dandridge Peck (1763–1822), of Harvard, wrote of the creature in the *Memoirs of the Academy of Arts & Sciences*. With the help of influential naturalist Samuel Mitchell (1841–94), Peck debunked the offspring monster as a common local variety of snake. After a time sightings trailed off.[9]

Few if any of the learned authors who wrote about the Cape Ann sea monster went to investigate for themselves. One of these was Revolutionary War hero, naturalist, and fellow of the Royal Society of London David Humphreys. Feeling the case important enough, Humphreys sent a series of letters on his adventure to Royal Society president Joseph Banks, for comment. Humphreys, "after several days fruitless search for the anomalous animal in question," analyzed what he had at hand.[10] To Humphreys, most of the eyewitnesses seemed like salt of the earth types who would not lie or exaggerate, so he took them seriously. He stated that the local revenue cutter—a government vessel—was taking on extra guns in case they should encounter the thing. As was common during this period, these letters were quickly compiled into a book. While ostensibly a scientific treatise on a newly discovered creature, Humphreys's book was written in a literary rather than a technical manner. This allowed him to include a plot line relating to American national pride. He saw the creature in terms of a monster from classical literature. He also made a challenge to his readers. "Who will dare to put," he asks grandly, "a hook in his nostrils, transfix his sides with a spear, or engage in single combat with Vulcanean arms this monarch of the deep, in his own element?"[11] He also thought that when captured the creature would show the grand design of God. The great serpent should remind people of the serpent in the Garden of Eden. Poetics aside, Humphreys admitted the evidence was still a bit thin on the ground, especially since the creature lived "in the dark and unfathomable abyss of ocean, among the unsearchable secrets of the GREAT DEEP."[12]

Eventually the Linnaean Society of New England had to admit that the baby sea monster discovered on shore was only a common snake. Their attempt to show the world their scientific skills did not work.[13] In 1861, sea monster author Philip Henry Gosse opined that he did not believe the Gloucester monster was real because Americans often make up tall tales and are unreliable when it comes to science.[14]

Despite the condescending attitude of some Europeans, a number of

American naturalists thought the creature did exist. One was Yale-educated Benjamin Silliman (1799–1864), one of the leading men of science in Early Republic America. He studied meteorites, was an early member of the fledgling American Association for the Advancement of Science, and edited the highly regarded *American Journal of Science*. American naturalists felt like poor relations next to their European counterparts, who generally regarded Americans as naive, impulsive, not as well educated as themselves, and generally producing inferior work. American science in the early decades of the nineteenth century had little respect or social status at home or abroad.[15]

Silliman and other American naturalists were eager to prove their mettle. Silliman, however, based his conclusions not on physical evidence, of which there was none, but on the veracity of the eyewitnesses. Naturalists were left with only discussions of the nature of sea serpents. None of the American naturalists who had come forward with opinions on the Cape Ann beast had ever seen it with their own eyes. Their only recourse was to study the witnesses. If eyewitnesses seemed beyond reproach, or had no reason to lie, had nothing to gain from reporting seeing a monster, they must be telling the truth. Such reports could be used to mask the absence of physical facts. The notion of reputable eyewitnesses as evidence for the existence of strange creatures became and still is a central issue for monster hunters (including those who chase the Jersey Devil). Making reliance upon eyewitnesses even more problematic, the nineteenth century in America was a time of widespread practical jokes and outright intellectual fraud.

Hoaxes in America

Next to the genuine monsters, such as the mammoth and hadrosaur, the American scene had room for many monsters, ghosts, and peculiar people. Journalists working in the burgeoning nineteenth-century American newspaper scene quickly realized the value of sensationalism. Natural disasters, outrageous crime, and strange human behavior boosted sales—monsters especially so. Anything out of the ordinary, whether based on facts or just as often not; indeed, any outré or prurient topic became fodder for newspapers as well as book publishers. The modern tabloid and "reality" media of the twenty-first century finds its origins here. During periods when no genuine odd events occurred, a journalist or editor could simply make them up.

One of the first major sensationalist media events of the post-revolutionary period came in the unlikely garb of the "Runaway Nuns." These women had lived in Catholic convents, usually under duress. The runaways variously claimed they had been beaten, sexually abused, or generally mistreated. This abuse came from priests and included out-of-wedlock pregnancies and murder. Individual women, such as Rebecca Reed, Josephine Bunkley, and most infamously Maria Monk, wrote books detailing their exploits at the hands of evil "Papists." Maria Monk's *Six Months in a Convent* (1834) proved so popular it sold more than 300,000 copies, making it the first modern bestseller in American publishing history.

The Runaway Nun phenomenon dovetailed with the rampant anti-Catholic movement in America. Protestants felt fearful of the increasing population of Catholic immigrants in the nation. They saw Catholics as suspect and secretive, all potential terrorists loyal to the Pope rather than the Republic. Many suspected that Catholics were involved in a grand conspiracy to overthrow the nation and turn it into a theocratic dictatorship under a strange and alien religious law. These fears were compounded by the Runaway Nun stories. Hysteria over their allegations led to a violent assault on a convent at Charlestown, outside Boston, which ended with the orphanage's burning. In 1871, New Jersey resident Edith O'Gorman published *Convent Life Unveiled*, in which she detailed the horrors that only ended when she "escaped" her convent. Tension between pro- and anti-Catholics ran so high over her allegations that when she gave a talk at a local Methodist church in Madison (just off the campus of Drew University), a riot broke out, with at least one pistol shot fired.

As anti-Catholic political leaders and media outlets embraced and promoted these women, some skeptics began to investigate. The strange narratives of the Runaway Nuns had many logical holes and outright falsehoods. Investigators quickly found these stories to be complete fabrications designed to stir up religious hatred.[16] Meanwhile, as Maria Monk told her harrowing tale of life in a convent, a fabulous story of life on the moon fought the nuns for tabloid space.

In 1832 the Briton Richard Adams Locke (a descendent of the philosopher John Locke) came to New York to make a name for himself as a journalist. He worked at one paper before landing a job as editor with the *Sun* in 1835. The *Sun*'s small circulation had been dwindling, and Locke began running a series of articles that changed the paper's fortunes. In 1826 a satirical article on the need to communicate with the possible sentient life forms on the moon had appeared in the *Edinburgh New Philosophical Journal*. Locke used it as an inspiration.

Locke understood that outrageous claims seemed more plausible if they were accompanied by technical jargon and the support of an authority. He reported on the work of the well-known astronomer Sir John Herschel, who was then in Cape Town, South Africa, having set up an observatory there. Herschel (1792–1871), son of astronomer Sir William Herschel—the dis-

One of the *Homo Vespertio* of Richard Adams Locke's Moon Hoax, which appeared in the *New York Sun* in 1835.

coverer of the planet Uranus—had constructed a large and sophisticated telescope that could see minute details on the surface of the moon. Locke said Herschel had been sending him reports of his lunar observations. Herschel had seen, Locke claimed, vegetation on the moon, including "the largest kind of Yews in an English garden." Animal life as well roamed the surface, including miniature bison and huge bipedal beavers. Most fantastically of all, Herschel had seen several different versions of human-like creatures that could fly, using large bat-like wings. Herschel called these creatures *Vespertilio homo*, the bat men.

These stories caused a sensation. The paper's readership exploded, and other papers reprinted his stories. A group of scientists from Yale University traveled to New York to see Locke, wanting to consult Herschel's letters. Eventually, the stories began to fall apart, and Locke was forced to admit the hoax. The story was believable partly because Herschel did have an observatory in South Africa. He had made important charts of the stars and observed the return of Halley's Comet. He did not, however, make any observations of the moon or life upon it, and he had not been sending breathless reports to Locke. Though the hoax had been exposed (Locke later claimed it was a satire rather than a hoax), Locke had shown that legitimacy could be gained for an outrageous story if "facts" and "authorities" could be mustered to support it.[17] The moon seemed to be populated with monstrous creatures and science confirmed it. The unmasking of the Moon Hoax did not deter newspaper editors from making up even more fantastic stories, nor did it stop readers from believing them.[18]

One did not have to go to the moon to find strange human-like creatures. Throughout the course of North American history there have been stories of the discovery of outsized men—literally giants—buried in the landscape. The most famous of these artifacts was the Cardiff Giant. Named for the New York State town near which it came to light, the Cardiff Giant attracted wide notice in 1869. Over nine feet tall, the strange discovery seemed uncannily human in its proportions and surface detail. Supposedly dug up by a farmer working his fields, the creature looked disturbingly like a giant naked man. After making a tidy sum charging the curious to see it, the farmer who claimed to have found it, William Newell, allowed several local naturalists to look at it. Othniel Charles Marsh (1831–99), a young Yale University paleontologist, was one of the first scientists to examine the hulking skeleton. Marsh was at the beginning of a long career as a public scientist and expert on dinosaurs. His training, and some common sense, allowed him to see the giant for what it was: a sculpture made of gypsum, not a human body.

The Cardiff Giant hoax had begun a year or so earlier, when a traveling cigar maker named George Hull—an outspoken atheist—became engaged in a raucous discussion about the Bible with an Evangelical preacher. Upset with what he considered unlettered, blind Christian faith, Hull hit upon the idea of testing Christian gullibility with some kind of hoax. Part of the argument centered on the biblical claim, in Genesis, that giants had existed in the past. He approached a stone mason in Iowa to create a heavy nine-foot-tall sculpture with human-like proportions. He then transported it to Cardiff, New York, not far from where he lived, and quietly buried it on the land of his cousin William Newell.

After waiting an appropriate length of time, Hull instructed Newell, who was in on the scheme, to go out and "find" the creature. Word of its discovery spread quickly, and soon crowds thronged the Newell farm. Charging fifty cents a head, Newell and Hull began raking in profits. This went on for some time, until O. C. Marsh called it a "humbug." The next day P. T. Barnum showed up. Impressed by the amount of cash being generated, Barnum tried to buy the Cardiff Giant, as it was now being called, but Hull and Newell refused to sell. Ever the enterprising and pragmatic business man, Barnum simply had a copy made and put it on display at his museum back in New York City. The public's appetite for giants and monsters was so strong that hucksters made copies and toured the country simultaneously.

Some years later another giant body was found, in California. Between 1895 and 1908 (just before the Jersey Devil story broke) news reports of the San Diego Giant made the rounds of the tabloids. A flurry of giant bodies turned up during this period. They were often supported by Christian Fundamentalists as proof that giants had "lived in the earth."[19] That there is no credible evidence of the remains of giant humans in North America is explained by the machinations of an ungodly and duplicitous government. The San Diego Giant story includes a reference to the Smithsonian Institution's being interested in obtaining the relic. The Smithsonian in particular and the US federal government in general were accused by conspiracy theorists of intentionally "suppressing" knowledge of such finds. The trope created by such theorists is that when a monstrous body is found, guileless civilians bring news of the find to the vaunted scientists. The evil scientists, wanting to protect their status as arbiters of knowledge and their precious theories, destroy any evidence of the discovery that giants indeed did live on the earth.

Many finds of human giants came in the form of disturbed Indian burials. They regularly took the form of two basic scenarios: someone "accidently" digs up an Indian grave and discovers an unnaturally large human skeleton, or a prospector enters a remote cave and then finds the freakish skeleton. Such discoveries are rarely made in Euro-American burial sites. The site is forgotten until a friend-of-a-friend-of-a-friend relates the tale, which winds up in the local newspaper. The physical evidence is never revealed, nor is the precise location of the find. Such discoveries and accusations made, and still make, popular fodder for tabloid newspapers. Indeed, newspaper editors contributed more to the strange and unusual in American history than did any other element.

Mermaids and Devils

Stories and illustrations of monsters went a long way to perpetrating a myth. Having a body to show people, however, could generate real revenue. One of the great monster hoaxes of the nineteenth century centered on the belief in mermaids. Since ancient times, stories about creatures half human and half fish have been common. In 1822 a British ship captain named Samuel Barnett Edes saw what he claimed was an actual captured mermaid body while in Japan. The preserved corpse, a kind of two-foot-long dried-out husk with a vaguely fishy body and a primate-like torso and head, belonged to some sailors. (The reality of supposed mermaid bodies never quite matched the beautiful woman-fish hybrid of male fantasies.) Determined to acquire it, Edes sold his ship—which actually belonged to the company he worked for— purchased the creature, and began to exhibit it. Furious, Edes's employers fired him and then began to pursue him for repayment. When he died, Edes left the creature to his son, who promptly sold it to a Boston man, Moses Kimball. In turn, Kimball showed the body to P. T. Barnum, who liked it so much he rented the creature and put it on display in 1842. It started Barnum on a history of acquiring—or faking—odd creatures and disfigured humans and exhibiting them to paying audiences.

Barnum prepared an entire backstory for what he now called the Feejee Mermaid. A British naturalist from a well-known British museum, Barnum claimed, had arrived in New York with the preserved body of a genuine siren he had discovered on the mysterious and exotic Pacific island of "Feejee." He produced a series of bogus letters that gave the creature provenance. He planted stories in various Philadelphia newspapers, whipping up a frenzy by the time he allowed people to see it in New York at his American Museum. Both the naturalist and his institution, as well as the letters, existed only in Barnum's creative imagination. Unfortunately, a fire at the New York museum destroyed the Feejee Mermaid. Unfazed, Barnum had another created and put that on display. The monster proved so popular that a number of exhibitors and sideshow entrepreneurs created their own mermaids and showed them with great success.[20]

While the popularity of Runaway Nuns, giants, and strange fossil animals show an enthusiasm for the bizarre in American culture, one hoax in particular bore an eerie resemblance to the Jersey Devil. In the late 1880s reports began to circulate around Cleveland, Ohio, of a curious birth. Dubbed "The Devil Kid," it was reputedly born to a "Polish family" in a working-class neighborhood of Newburg. It carried a number of the same frightening characteristics later associated with the Jersey Devil: reddish skin, horns, claws and hooves, and a long pointy tail. The story also fed into anti-immigrant sentiment. The Devil Kid even had its own catchphrase. Whereas Mother Leeds had yelped, "Oh, let this one be a Devil!" as she delivered the creature, the attending doctor in the Devil Kid story blurted out "Great God, but we must kill the thing!" News reports referred to this monstrosity as "Satan incarnate." After creating a stir, there was not much more for the Devil Kid to do, so newspapermen killed it off after a relatively short life span. Unlike the creature of the Pine Barrens, the Devil Kid, a more urban version, did not haunt the woods attacking people. The "body" of the Devil Kid, however, circulated in traveling displays for a time across Ohio, Pennsylvania, and New York. It would have been known by the Philadelphia newspapermen who cobbled together the Jersey Devil story.[21] Parading the bodies of monsters such as the Devil Kid occurred quite often and proved popular with the public, further supporting the idea that such creatures did actually exist.

Closer to home, in December 1885, Elizabeth, New Jersey, found itself plagued by an ominous ghost-like creature. Reported at over twelve feet tall, this otherworldly being had glowing eyes and horns. It had the capability to lunge over tall fences, run up the sides of buildings, and flit through the tops of trees. Noiseless, it pursued women in an attempt to embrace and kiss them. Referred to as "Spring Heeled Jack," for its climbing and jumping abilities, the creature genuinely frightened people. It seemed to frequent St. Michael's Church on East Jersey Street. The name *Spring Heeled Jack* first appeared in Victorian London as a moniker of a frightening devil-like creature that accosted and assaulted pedestrians in that great city.[22] The year before, stories about the British Spring Heeled Jack appeared in newspapers from New York to Kansas to Montana, and was well known in America.[23]

Terrible, almost supernatural assailants seemed to be everywhere during the late nineteenth century. Starting with Jack the Ripper in London, a "Jack the Cutter" terrorized Philadelphia, attacking women in 1899. He would sneak up on them and then slash their clothes. Across America one could find "Jack the Kisser," "Jack the Hugger," and "Jack the Stone Thrower." Newspapers in the Middle Atlantic region carried reports of all these activities. When the Leeds Devil morphed into the Jersey Devil, it did not do so as an isolated event but as part of a well-established tradition. It did not walk alone but in the company of a veritable parade of strange villains.

A Monster Is Born

Legend often lists Daniel and Mother Leeds as the parents of the Jersey Devil; however, that title better belongs to a group of twentieth-century Philadelphia entrepreneurs rather than an eighteenth-century witch. Indeed, by the early nineteenth century (if not earlier), the original colonial Leeds family and their history had faded from view except for occasional mentions. What was left was the Leeds Devil, a vague and ill-defined creature of the forest. A legend made up of parts from religious and political quarrels mixed with Native American folklore and half-remembered stories from Europe had replaced the Leeds family. As in all good magic acts, no one saw the switch take place.

The final act of that obliteration came at the hands of hucksters. These men took the all but forgotten colonial era Leeds Devil and rebranded it.

The legend—never that widespread to begin with—stood on the verge of extinction at the end of the nineteenth century. Only a few mentions appear during the nineteenth century, the most outlandish of these being that a rare appearance by the monster had presaged the outbreak of the Civil War (though this assertion came after that conflict was over).

The original haunts of the Leeds family had changed as well. Once a vibrant center of religious practice, political thought and activity, even of cosmopolitan outlook, the Pine Barrens and the town of Burlington slipped into a kind of reclusiveness, overtaken by Philadelphia and New York. Like an old shack teetering on the edge of disintegration but refusing to finally topple over, the Leeds Devil story refused to vanish completely. Some of the rural inhabitants of the Pine Barrens region—known ungraciously as "Pineys"—still held the legend in some regard. W. F. Mayer's 1859 article showed how the perception of the people of the Pine Barrens had changed over time. In Daniel Leeds's day, the area towns pulsed with life. By the middle of the nineteenth century, however, that image had evolved. Some saw the thick forests as home to stereotypical, dull-witted bumpkins, wary of outsiders and none too friendly.[24] The Jersey Devil legend gets a good bit of its steam from this perception of the Pineys as ragged, near savages engaged in who-knows-what in their darkened lairs and rude hovels. Such a location made for an admirable place to birth a monster.

In 1884, as Spring Heeled Jack was terrorizing Elizabeth, the original biblical Devil made an appearance in the Garden State. Members of an African American church claimed to have seen the Evil One hovering about. The correspondent for the Washington, DC, *National Republican* jibed that "New Jersey is probably the only state in the Union where such a thing could happen."[25] Devils in the woods of New Jersey were fit only for the incredulous, the backward, and the deluded. Another late-nineteenth-century devil story from the Pine Barrens involves an instrument maker and musician named Sam Giberson (1808–84), who boasted he could play the fiddle better than the devil. In a classic "deal with the devil" scenario, he creates a song called an "air tune," so obscure no one can play it.[26]

In 1893 one of the most popular incidents of the Leeds Devil mythos hit the media. An Erie Railroad engineer claimed that he and his train had come under attack by the creature. The thing scared him badly because, he said, "the face was like that of an ape or monkey." When someone asked if he had not been startled by a large owl flying past his train cab, he replied indignantly, "By——! That hain't no owl; that's the Leeds Devil! Back ag'in, sure as you're livin!" This account also claimed that the creature had originated in Evansham Woods and that there had been a religious cleansing of the creature that would keep it away for a hundred years. That period was now up, which accounted for the creature's reappearance. It was, the article stated, all the fault of a man named Leeds and his demonic wife, who had cursed her own child as well as the day she had married.[27]

A sighting in 1899 brought renewed vitality to the legend when the creature appeared to two men in the forest. This account drew on the element of the hundred-year banishment of the creature. This allowed for an explanation as to why few stories about the Leeds Devil had circulated. People had not lost interest in the Leeds Devil; it simply hadn't appeared, because a Christian ritual had kept it suppressed. The author said the banishment rumor began with "some old wiseacre" saying that a "pious man" might "exercise an enchantment and banish the Evil One for one hundred years." Who this "pious man" turned out to be did not get recorded, or when, specifically, he performed the exorcism, though internal logic seemed to suggest some time in the later eighteenth century. This author also felt obliged to remind his readers—as the story had so fallen from the popular imagination—of the details of the Leeds Devil. The creature had issued from Mother Leeds with cloven hoofs and bat wings; it ate children and prophesized major catastrophes. "In New Jersey folklore," he said, the creature "is analogous to the werewolf of German mountaineers, but more hideous and more fantastical." He went on to say that "a number of collections of family manuscripts" of the post-revolutionary era make reference to it, though again he does not cite specific cases, and no such collections have ever been located.[28] A month after this article appeared in St. Paul, Minnesota, an Akron, Ohio, paper reprinted it with the title "Jersey Sees a Devil."[29]

By the early years of the twentieth century, the Leeds Devil story's energy had dissipated enough that author Charles Montgomery Skinner, in his *American Myths and Legends* (1903), stated with some finality that the Leeds Devil "had become a dim tradition." Skinner wrapped up what he thought was a quaint old tale for the last time. He recounted that it had appeared, in good monster tradition, just before various wars, fires, and other calamities. He assumed believers saw the story in the classic medieval and Early Modern period mold as a vehicle of prophesy. Restating the old tales and rumors, he noted that Mother Leeds, though "a sober Quaker in appearance," was in fact a diabolical witch. He also resurrected the story that in the 1740s a clergyman "with candle, book, and bell . . . banned the creature for a hundred years." As in all previous accounts, Skinner too gives no details of who this "clergyman" was and ignores the fact that Quaker clergy did not perform exorcisms. He lists what will become the standard "facts" about the creature: born in 1735, with bat-like wings, pigs' feet à la Martin Luther's

Monk Calf monster, and responsible for the disappearance of children. His review of the relevant literature suggested to him that few sightings had cropped up after 1840 and then only intermittently. Skinner somewhat condescendingly concluded that "many worshipful commoners of Jersey dismissed for good and all, the fear of this monster from their minds."[30] Not long after Skinner wrote with such confidence that the Leeds Devil was dead, this all but forgotten tradition suddenly burst into sharp, bright focus.

A Myth Created

While the story of the Leeds Devil had occasionally made it into newspapers outside of New York, New Jersey, and Pennsylvania, its content excited little more than mild curiosity. That changed in 1905, two years after Skinner had laid it to rest, when a fleshed-out rendering of the modern variation of the story appeared in the *Trenton Times*. Similar to the monster seen by the train engineer in 1893, the creature described by the *Trenton Times* was a monkey-like thing, did not immediately fly off after birth, but lived with the family for some years before finally disappearing into the woods in 1808. The wife, local gossip said, "associated her name with beings of the other world." After her first child had been born in some difficulty, she cursed her second child (which turned out to be the monster) before it was conceived. While most at the time believed the birthplace of the monster to be in the vicinity of Leeds Point, the author of the article, Alminus Alba, claimed otherwise. With some specificity he says that Mother Leeds gave birth to her monstrous progeny in Bordentown, in a house on the "Northeastern corner of Farnsworth Avenue and McKnight's Alley." The owner of the house was Parmelia Jolly. The account suggests vaguely that Ms. Jolly suffered ill effects from her connection to the infamous location. She was buried in the "Baptist section of the graveyard on Church Street."[31] During this period the creature alternately came to be called the Leeds Devil, Leeds Satan, Flying-Hoof, Air-Hos (horse), and Winged Dog. Oddly, though the article described the monster as being simian, the accompanying illustrations show the now familiar dragon configuration. These tellings reduced the entire Leeds family down to "Captain Leeds" and his demonic wife, "Mother Leeds," while moving the events to the early nineteenth century.

These articles were prompted in part because that winter strange, unrecognizable footprints had appeared in the snow in the Pine Barrens. Vague whispers began to circulate about the old legends of the Leeds Devil. This time the cosmic gears turned just the right way, and interest in the story gained steam. By early 1909, an important year for the Devil, several Philadelphia newspapers ran accounts of more "curious hoof-prints made . . . by some strange animal not yet classified by scientist or nature-faker," in the snows around Bordentown, Mount Holly, and Leeds Point. The *Trenton Evening Times* included a series of humorous cartoons to go with their article, showing a reptilian, dragon-like figure with leathery wings, clawed hands, and hooved feet.[32] Other newspapers then picked up on the legend. The Leeds Devil newspaper reports began to increase. Like any celebrity phenomenon, it needed a professional to craft a media-savvy image.

Walking back to his office in the bitter cold of January, Philadelphia promotions man Norman Jeffries read the local newspaper. He saw the reports of the strange tracks and the mention of the Leeds Devil. His steps quickened. Stories about a forgotten monster might just be the thing to save his boss's business and his own job.

Norman Jeffries burst into the office of his boss, Charles A. Bradenburgh. He told him and business manager T. F. Hopkins about the legend. He showed them the newspapers, then told them the scheme he had formulated during his walk over. Any other business owner might have looked askance at Jeffries, questioned his sanity, or even fired him. This however, was no ordinary business, this was the Ninth and Arch Street Dime Museum, and whacky ideas, crazy stunts, and outright shenanigans were their stock in trade. They all smelled an opportunity to cash in and save their struggling enterprise.

Another element that aided the return of the Leeds Devil in the sensationalist press was the growing sense of American prosperity. Following the economic slump of the post–Civil War era, the American economy grew so rapidly that Mark Twain dubbed it the Gilded Age. The period of the Indian Wars had made it safer for settlers to travel west, and the expansion of the transcontinental railroad system made travel easier and more efficient. The Industrial Revolution had made a more prosperous middle class, which could spend money on frivolities such as newspapers, theater, and other amusements, often dealing with the strange and unusual. The combination of high-speed printing and the appetite for the weird meant that editors needed material to put in their papers.

Dime museums such as the Ninth and Arch were popular centers of lowbrow entertainment in the late nineteenth and early twentieth centuries. They brought unusual and outrageous performers and spectacles to working-class and middle-class audiences that were looking for cheap thrills. Along with such traditional performers as singers, musicians, actors, and acrobats, less conventional acts—fat women and living skeletons—appeared.[33] One of the more popular performance spaces was the New Dime Museum in Philadelphia, originally opened in 1869. In 1884 Charles A. Bradenburgh became

This might be considered the "classic" image of the Jersey Devil, an emaciated flying horse. It appeared in the *Philadelphia Bulletin* in 1909.

the proprietor of the establishment, and because of its location he renamed it the Ninth and Arch Street Dime Museum. Bradenburgh, "well known for his business qualifications," had been in show business in different management capacities for years.[34] (Bradenburgh also became the owner of the large iconic elephant-shaped building at Coney Island, New York.) The museum had been closed, but when Bradenburgh reopened it, he made sure to let people know it had been improved to assure the visitor's safety as well as enjoyment. "It has been handsomely fitted up," the *Philadelphia Inquirer* boasted, "and provided with better ventilation and better modes of egress." Live performances, such as "A Pair of Kids" and "The Banker's Luck," would appear alongside exotic acts like Laloo the Chinese acrobat.[35]

The term *museum* was employed rather loosely for such establishments as the Ninth and Arch. The intention of the word's usage meant to give them a veneer of respectability. In reality such institutions looked more like permanent circus sideshows. The lower floor of the Ninth and Arch resembled a later-century penny arcade. The second floor held the animal acts, and the third floor showcased human anomalies and performers. Along with the sword swallowers, illusionists, games of chance, and freaks, Bradenburgh brought in the latest novelty: motion pictures. Something of a visionary in this regard, Bradenburgh early on grasped the money-making potential of showing cinema. Despite his best efforts, however, Bradenburgh's museum struggled. He needed something to get the crowds in.[36] This is why Bradenburgh only leaned back in his chair and smiled when Jeffries told of his idea. His best was yet to come.

By 1908 Bradenburgh had employed Hopkins as manager and Jeffries as press agent. Eager for any outlandish scheme to bring paying rubes into the museum, and showing no scruples about honesty or accuracy, Jeffries began to plant stories in the local press about the Leeds Devil and its sinister behavior. These early January 1909 newspaper articles were read by an eager public already interested in the reports of the footprints in the snow. It is these newspaper accounts—for the Jersey Devil is a product of the media rather than genuine folklore—that began the birthing process. The *Trenton Evening News* exclaimed on its front page that the "Leeds Devil has Jersey People Frightened."[37] The scheme had the desired effect, even though they did not actually have anything to show. Attendance at the museum and the circulation of the newspapers carrying the stories grew. The *New York Tribune* asked if anybody doubted the stories of tracks in the snow now that they had been confirmed.[38] A new moniker caught on quickly as well. As far away as Minnesota a headline exclaimed "Real 'Jersey Devil' Found."[39]

Sometime later Jeffries, basking in the glow of his inspired success, found himself confronted by the editor of a newspaper that had not run his stories. He told Jeffries he knew the entire thing was a prank and strongly suggested he should end it and "kill off" the creature. Jeffries and Bradenburgh saw one last chance to capitalize on the Leeds Devil story. Familiar with the careers of the Feejee Mermaid and the Cardiff Giant (both had been covered in the Philadelphia and New York press), Bradenburgh and Jeffries knew that nothing packed them in like an actual body. If a mermaid and a giant could be constructed out of dead fish parts and stone and make their exhibitors rich, why not a devil? The Philadelphia showmen contacted local taxidermist Jacob Hope, who in turn contacted Buffalo, New York, animal trainer and exhibitor "Professor Edwards," who supplied them with the closest thing he could think of to what the museum men described. A few days later a live kangaroo quietly arrived in the City of Brotherly Love. Hope painted stripes on the kangaroo and attached a pair of homemade wings to the poor creature's back. Jeffries then hired a Ringling Brothers Circus clown named George Hartzell and some of his friends to act as monster hunters and go out on an "expedition" to catch the fiendish beast. This event may very well

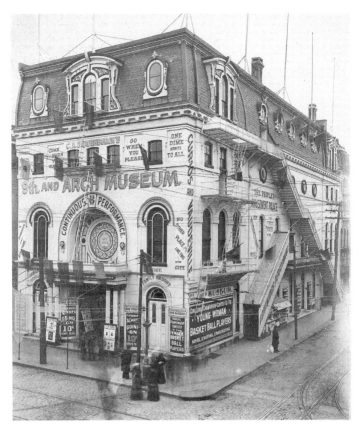

The Ninth and Arch Street Dime Museum in Philadelphia—the actual birthplace of
the Jersey Devil. Free Library of Philadelphia, Print and Picture Collection.

be the first such excursion in American history. With some fanfare the group
headed off into the woods to capture the monster that had for so long frightened the people of Pennsylvania and New Jersey. After disappearing into the
dark forest. those left behind heard desperate shouts and gunshots. Screams
of men and a strange beast could be heard. After this pulse-quickening encounter the group reemerged. The effects of the battle could be seen in the
men's faces. They brought with them on a cart, however, a blanket-covered
cage. As they manhandled the cart into town the cage rattled and shook, on
occasion with unnerving screeches emanating from some blasphemous beast
locked inside. The group repaired to the museum with the quarry. The next
day the papers claimed that the Leeds Devil had been captured and was
now on display at the Ninth and Arch Street Dime Museum. It caused just

the sort of sensation the proprietors had hoped for. Crowds began to swarm the theater, and the museum "collected thousands of dollars from curious spectators."[40]

People flocked to the Ninth and Arch Street Dime Museum, paid their admission and caught a brief performance of the "monster." Situated on a darkened stage, the curtain-covered cage sat just close enough to the edge to be seen, but not touched, should any brave soul suddenly reach out to grab at it. The covering pulled back, the horrid thing appeared. Unseen by the crowd a young boy wielding a long stick with a nail in it hidden in the stage curtains would poke the beast making it shout, yelp, and jump around. The audience roared with fright while bells clanged and the "monster" tried to flee its cage. The hoax had been taken to the extreme, but it worked well for the promoter and extended the legend of what was increasingly being called the Jersey Devil. It appears likely that the kangaroo used for this trick influenced many of the people who later thought they saw a flying kangaroo, including one known as a "Jabberwock."[41]

To some, the jig was up. Journalistic wags gleefully spilled the beans that the entire Jersey Devil episode was a colossal hoax.[42] After several weeks of packed audiences the crowds began to agree, and Bradenburgh and company saw that the ruse had run its course. They washed the paint off the kangaroo, clipped its wings, and sent the hapless creature back to Professor Edwards in Buffalo. This performance turned out to be Bradenburgh and Jeffries's swan song. Despite the success of the Jersey Devil hoax, the museum closed. Its owner was later referred to as "the man in whose interest the greatest hoax ever conceived by a press agent was perpetrated," while Jeffries found himself labeled "a diabolical press agent" for creating the hoax.[43]

However, the work of the Philadelphia hucksters now took on a life of its own. Sightings of the Jersey Devil began to come in from a number of sources. The Pine Barrens rattled with Jersey Devils in 1909. At least two hunts took place during this period, and several bodies were said to have been found. Monster hunters out of Bloomsbury, Pennsylvania, tried to enlist the help of the local authorities. Bloomsbury chief of police Tommy Walker wisely declined any official assistance and preferred to stay in town doing the job he felt he was being paid to do.[44] At the same time as the Bloomsbury hunt, an intrepid Jersey shore fisherman encountered the creature at sea off the coastal town of Brigantine. Captain George Doughty claimed his boat had come under attack by a giant bird-like creature that he fended off with an oar. Was this, the news account breathlessly exclaimed, "the much-discussed Jersey Devil which excited South Jersey several months ago?"[45] On Halloween in Virginia the news media claimed that such a creature, only twenty inches long, did indeed exist, but that it had been killed.[46]

Conclusion

The ending of the exhibit of the Jersey Devil at The Ninth and Arch Street Dime Museum and the revelation that it had all been a hoax should have ended the story. It did not. The notion of a demonic part-horse, part-bat dragon with hooves and claws, born of an occult-practicing human mother, struck a chord. People who had seen the creature in its cage, as well as those who never entered the museum, began to claim they had seen it in the wild. The twentieth century would see waves of sightings of twisted equine bodies moving menacingly through the woods, leaping over streams and houses, and engaging in a wide range of unnerving activities, which would continue into the twenty-first century. The quiet, foreboding Pine Barrens, with its thick woods, dim glades, reclusive inhabitants, and imposing solitude, had finally produced a monster. Regardless of whether it was dead or alive or how large or small or real it was, the Jersey Devil had been born. Ironically, just as legend held that the Leeds Devil had escaped from the Leeds family, the Jersey Devil escaped its Philadelphia parents, found refuge in the forest, and was now ready to haunt the dreams of a new generation.

The Devil's Biographers

D ESPITE THE VARIOUS SIGHTINGS of the Jersey Devil in the early twentieth century, there was little attempt to analyze the legend. Newspaper reports took the form of breathless descriptions of encounters and speculative retellings of the story of Mother Leeds and her awful child. It was not until the 1930s that a few writers tried to piece together the legend without overly sensationalizing it. A cadre of genealogists and amateur local historians began to write about the Jersey Devil. While they did not create it, these authors did much to propagate the fable. Though they spurned modern historical methods and were too easy to accept outrageous legends, they became the inspiration for later authors, internet bloggers, monster hunters, and film and video makers.

It is commonly thought that reports of the Jersey Devil go back to the colonial era. A reputed description of the Leeds Devil comes from the supposed diary of West Jersey resident Vance Larner, dated 1790.[1] This reference, however, is of dubious provenance, so must be discounted.[2] The Vance Larner Diary has been referred to in several stories about the Jersey Devil in the twentieth century. Its riveting account of the apparition in the pines is repeated by authors and in popular new accounts. In this description the myth is emboldened and detailed. "It was neither beast nor man nor spirit," Larner claims to have said, "but a hellish brew of all three. . . . It was dashing its tail to and fro in the pond and rubbing its horns against a tree trunk. . . . It was as large as a moose with leather wings."[3] Unfortunately, the Larner diary is a likely a hoax, with no physical or textural evidence supporting its existence.

By contrast, there are several contemporary books written about life in the Jerseys in the eighteenth century. Books by Samuel Smith and Pehr Kalm, for example, include extensive sections on flora and fauna. None of them describes a creature even remotely resembling the Leeds Devil, in reality or in legend.[4]

The earliest confirmed mention of the Leeds Devil in print comes in W. F. Mayer's article for the *Atlantic Monthly*, which appeared in May 1859. A journalist, Mayer traveled to southern New Jersey in order to write about the culture of the inhabitants of the Pine Barrens, a region he called "aboriginal in [its] savagery."[5] Mayer viewed the "Pine Rats" as barely human in their squalid living conditions, referring to them as "the degraded descendants of Torries . . . completely besotted and brutish in their ignorance." "They are," he continued, "incapable of obtaining an honest living" and thus survive by stealing and other forms of general knavery.[6]

During his jaunt in the Pine Barrens, Mayer met with a local woman named Hannah Butler. He described her as overtly unpleasant, speaking in a guttural voice and living with her equally revolting nephew in a broken-down tent in the middle of the woods. The pair was clearly aware of the monster legend, that it had existed for some time, and they feared the beast. While chit-chatting about the weather, Mrs. Butler offhandedly remarked that the coming storm would be like the one that occurred the night "when I seed [sic] the Leeds' Devil." Mayer's interest was piqued, but before he could ask any more questions or get any more information out of her, the nephew nervously shushed her, and the tatty pair shambled off. Mayer's local guide later spelled out to him what has become the standard story of the Leeds Devil. In 1735 Mother Leeds gave birth to a dragon-like creature, which went on to haunt the woods. "Little children," he said, "did be eaten and maids abused." Mayer put down Hannah's fear of the creature to her alcoholism and prickly personality. The story, as far as he was concerned, was just another example of the depraved, backward, and superstitious nature of the Pine Rats.[7]

After Mayer's article in the *Atlantic Monthly* in 1859, the next newspaper accounts to include references to the Leeds Devil do not appear until the 1880s. The first, from 1887, asserts that the creature was born in Evesham, New Jersey, just outside Burlington. A young scion of the Leeds family married a local girl from a good family, but of dubious decorum. She enjoyed attending parties and husking-bees and other merriments more than the duties of married life. When she became pregnant she grew upset and apparently made her husband's life difficult. While giving birth to her first child she cried out, "Oh, let it be a devil." When the hideous beast emerged it shot up the chimney and disappeared into the woods. This version also included the detail that someone had fired silver bullets at the creature without effect.[8] The second article, from 1893, recounts the story of the New Jersey engineer who claimed the creature had attacked him while he drove his train, frightening him. He was sure that he had been attacked by the Leeds Devil.[9]

The first person to begin collecting material on the Leeds/Jersey Devil legend with an eye toward telling its full story was Philadelphia-born lawyer Francis Bazley Lee (1869–1914). Lee worked as the clerk for the New Jersey Supreme Court, but his real passion was New Jersey history. He wrote and edited a number of books on genealogy and compiled material on the Leeds Devil story. Unfortunately, he published none of this work, and most of it was lost after his death.[10] Lee edited the multivolume *Genealogical and Memorial History of the State of New Jersey* (1910), which contains a brief section on the Leeds family. It includes a meager biography of Daniel Leeds, but nothing on monsters.[11] Some of Lee's research on the Jersey Devil made it to print in the smallest of ways through an article by his acquaintance J. Elfreth Watkins, titled "Demon of the Pines," published in 1905, the year Leeds Devil mania began.[12]

Watkins (1852–1903), an engineer, railroad executive, and later Smithsonian Institution curator of the history of technology and transportation, dabbled in futuristic predictions (with some prescience) and had an interest in odd folklore. In the December 1900 issue of *Lady's Home Journal* Watkins predicted round-the-world telephone service, rapid transport between the United States and the United Kingdom, and a number of other technological innovations that have since come to be.[13] Like Lee, Watkins wrote a brief article that found its way into the *Washington Evening Star*. Half the article centered on snake collectors of the Pine Barrens and the other half on the Leeds Devil.[14] Watkins's version of the tale says Mother Leeds was a witch, and her offspring was more dragon than child. The father was the Devil himself. Watkins includes the scene of the creature frightening the people in attendance at its birth before flying up the chimney. He also included what may be the first reference to Joseph Bonaparte and Steven Decatur being active participants in the legend. Decatur, Watkins claimed, fired cannonballs at the creature, and Bonaparte saw it flying around his New Jersey estate.

Watkins's article was the second published in 1905 intended to provide a historical context for the legend. The first appeared in July in the *Trenton Times*, by Arminius Alba, who laid out most of the major Jersey Devil motifs, along with a few that were not part of the canon. Described here as a monkey-like creature rather than a dragon, the newborn monster does not immediately fly away after birth but lives with the family for some years before doing its dramatic exit up the chimney. This Leeds family is headed by a Captain Leeds and his wife, and the events occur in 1808 rather than 1735. The wife, local gossip said, was an alleged sorceress, who "associated her name with beings of the other world."[15] The article included a series of humorous cartoons that, despite the text making reference to primate morphology, shows a dragon-like figure with leathery wings, clawed hands, and hooved feet. It is in the Mayer article of 1859, along with the 1905 articles and the publicity stunts of the Ninth and Arch Dime Museum, that the modern Jersey Devil legend came into focus. Aside from the tabloid press, the most widely known research into the story of the Jersey Devil began with the work of journalist turned folklorist turned Episcopalian priest Henry Charlton Beck.

Henry Charlton Beck and His Offspring

For modern monster aficionados the work Francis Bazley Lee and of John Elfreth Watkins remained largely unknown. The canon text for Jersey Devil studies came in the work of Henry Charlton Beck (1902–65). While waiting for his ordination as an Episcopalian priest, Beck worked as a journalist in Camden. He developed a passion for the obscure town histories of New Jersey and produced a series of books about them. He dreamily wandered the back roads of New Jersey talking with local people, filling notebook after notebook with their tales and recollections. Though not a monster or ghost hunter, Beck would eventually include material on the Leeds/Jersey Devil in some of his books.

In 1937 Beck published *More Forgotten Towns of Southern New Jersey*. He mentioned the colonial era Leeds family and noted that Daniel Leeds had published almanacs as well as a book titled *The Temple of Wisdom*, that his work constituted the earliest publishing in New Jersey, and that he had served as councilor to the governor, Lord Cornbury. However, Beck stated incorrectly that Benjamin Franklin mentions Daniel Leeds in *Poor Richard's Almanac* when Franklin's reference was, in fact, to Titan Leeds. Beck did not mention the Jersey Devil in this book and apparently had no idea of its connection to the Leeds family; he mentions the Leeds family only as the founders of the town of Leeds Point.[16]

An amateur folklorist and journalist, Beck eschewed the historian's search for verifiable facts and evidence. Indeed, he had the amateur's distaste for professionals, referring to the works of historical scholars derisively as "dry as dust." His preference was for atmosphere, romance, and charm. Written in an engaging, conversational style, his books are as much about his personal experience unearthing New Jersey folklore as the folklore itself, which he collected from a series of colorful characters. He transcribed oral traditions for their own sake, not out of an attempt to accurately reconstruct history. This makes his work problematic for later researchers. He gives no citations or footnotes to where his material comes from other than saying his interviewees (whom he names only occasionally) told him. His bibliography is short and fragmentary, making his work all but useless as an historical reference.

Beck's major discussion of Jersey Devil lore came in *Jersey Genesis* (1945), where he again mentions Daniel Leeds and his colonial family as compilers of almanacs, but makes no direct connection to the Leeds Devil legend or the Titan Leeds feud with Benjamin Franklin. What Beck does is copy out the Leeds Devil section of John Elfreth Watkins's "Demon of the Pines" article. Unfortunately, Beck's lack of and distaste for historical protocol is so acute that while he does give credit to Watkins, he misquotes the title of the article. Beck calls it "On the Trail of the Leeds Devil." He conflates Watkins's work with an unrelated article from 1918 titled "On the Trail of the Jersey Devil."[17] These issues make one of the founding texts of Jersey Devil studies deeply flawed. Beck's intellectual descendants have passed along his mistakes as authoritative gospel. As a result, later researchers, authors, and monster hunters had little if any knowledge of the important roles played by Daniel Leeds, Titan Leeds, Benjamin Franklin, the Quakers, and the religious and political strife of the colonial era. Beck, by leaving these elements out of the story almost completely (if he even knew of them) contributed to the disappearance of the early Leeds family, and the loss of the origins of the legend, from the historical record. While he made no mention of him, details Beck listed indicate that he also used W. F. Mayer's 1859 article as a source text, as did Francis Bazley Lee. Beck became the focal point of Jersey Devil studies as he codified all the work done before him into a single corpus. With few exceptions, later authors seemed uninterested in looking beyond what Beck had written; they were content to simply copy his work. They also were content to quote newspaper articles from the period without exploring the underlying sources or determining whether or not the authors were embellishing for effect.

At about the same time, the United States federal government involved itself in the story. In 1939, as part of the New Deal, the WPA-sponsored book on New Jersey was released. It made several references to the creature as both the Leeds Devil and Jersey Devil. Taking a decidedly tongue-in-cheek approach, it referenced several sightings from the period. It makes no mention of the colonial Leeds family or the political and religious turmoil from which the legend sprang. It does offhandedly refer to the creature as "the official state demon."[18]

Based upon this foundation, the later secondary literature on the Jersey Devil legend creates more obstacles than it removes. The vast majority of publications and websites simply rehash the material found in Beck and the early-twentieth-century media reports, making little attempt to check sources. During the twentieth century, almost anything attributed to the Jersey Devil made it into the larger myth. Later reports of children killed by the creature or an attempt by local clergy to "exorcise" the Devil in the eighteenth century have no supporting documentation in the historical record (also, Quakers did not perform exorcisms). James F. McCloy and Ray Miller Jr's *The Jersey Devil* (1976) offers no footnotes, a bibliography of less than half a page, and a simple list of newspapers consulted, with no references to specific articles.[19] In *South Jersey Towns* (1973), William McMahon claims that folklorist Fred MacFadden found references to the Leeds Devil beginning in 1735, but neither author published a citation or reference supporting this claim, so it cannot be checked.[20] Even in the twenty-first century, books and television documentaries are regularly turned out with little or no citations or references to sources.[21]

Primary sources can also be misleading when restricted to media reports on the creature itself. Surveys of extant newspapers of the colonial and Early Republic period have turned up no references to any of the story's characters in relationship to the production of a monster. The bulk of reports of the creature do not begin until the turn of the twentieth century. These sources all but ignore the real life family that came to be attached to the legend. Other primary sources, however, do add useful material: the Leeds-produced almanacs and other ephemera. It is here that the origins of the Jersey Devil can be found. The traces of this myth are left in the pamphlets and tracts of the region rather than in monstrous footprints.

Daniel Leeds himself, the unintentional progenitor of the story, shows up only sporadically in the modern historiography of America. He has been all but written out of Quaker history. Charles F. Heartman's privately printed bibliography of almanacs, *Preliminary Checklist of Almanacs Printed in New Jersey Prior to 1850* (1929), for example, never mentions the Leeds almanacs or other works, starting his list in 1760.[22] Likewise, Joseph J. Felcone's extensive *Printing in New Jersey: 1754–1800* (2012) begins his history well after the heyday of the Leeds family. Felcone's interest is in printers and permanent presses rather than publishers and authors, so this may account for the absence.[23] Leeds appears in brief biographical entries in publications such as the *Dictionary of American Biography* and in a few nineteenth-century local histories of New Jersey. Their lives had become hazy enough that an 1848 newspaper article on the history of almanacs in New Jersey incorrectly stated that the Franklin/Leeds feud had occurred in 1773.[24] This dissipation of memory had so set in that by 1900, in his *Daily Union History of Atlantic County*, author John F. Hall incorrectly called Daniel Leeds "the writer of the single volume called the *Book of Wisdom* [sic]."[25] This was copied by the biographer of the Leeds family, genealogist Clara Louise Humeston, and later Leeds family chronicler Alfred M. Heston, in an article for the *Proceedings of the New Jersey Historical Society*.[26]

Another consideration for the lack of mention of Daniel Leeds is that while he wrote numerous books and pamphlets, few of them physically survive. A few repositories have microfilm versions, but not originals. Only one copy of his first book, *The Temple of Wisdom* (1688), exists, as does *News of a Strumpet* (1701).[27] Some of his original work can be found in Oxford University's Bodleian Library or the British Library. The very nature of almanacs was that they were meant to be used for a given year, after which they were often discarded. In addition, some of Leeds's Quaker neighbors found his work so objectionable they actively sought to destroy it, in America and in England.

The Devil's Reign

Despite the spurious nature of the reports, the 1909 panic became a case of mass hysteria. Fear of the devil caused people in the pines to stay indoors and obey curfews. Some joined hunting parties. When public officials and police began to claim they had seen the monster, complete public pandemonium ensued. A Burlington policeman, never identified, evidently saw the Jersey Devil and identified it as the "Jabberwock," from Lewis Carroll's poem *Jabberwocky*, meaning "nonsensical speech or writing that appears to make sense."[28] Like its fictional counterpart, the New Jersey "Jabberwock" was said to have eyes like "blazing coals" and "no teeth." The creature was reputed to have next flown to Collingswood, then on to Morristown. One of the onlookers said it even looked like a "winged kangaroo."[29] These sightings came and went over the course of the twentieth century and led to the appearance of those who wanted to tell the Jersey Devil's story and to those who wanted to capture the devil alive.

Alleged sightings of the Jersey Devil continued to occur for years after 1909. The number of sightings decreased in the period from 1921 to 1950, though interest did not. Searches for the creature began to take place. Newspaper articles had so played up the tracks in the snow that by 1929 a posse of local people set out to capture the beast.[30] A 1930 article in the *New York Times* referred to the Jersey Devil's return after a period of inactivity.[31] Odd marks, or "Devil's footprints," had been reported in the British Isles for centuries before the story of the Jersey Devil, and such tracks had been vaguely associated with the Leeds Devil since the mid-nineteenth century. Many of the 1905–9 reports said that tracks had been found in the snow. These tracks seemed horse-like, yet different. Also, some of these mysterious tracks appeared in places—for example, on rooftops—where horses would not have gone. The shape, distance, and abruptness of these tracks led to speculation that the Jersey Devil could fly, supporting the dragon-like horse with wings model.[32]

As happens with many legends, historic personages having no connection to the original events become caught up in the mythology. The exiled king of Spain, Joseph Bonaparte, who was the brother of Napoleon Bonaparte, found himself dragged into the Jersey Devil legend. While living in exile in the early 1800s at his estate, Point Breeze, in Bordentown, Joseph allegedly sighted the devil while hunting.[33] No shots were fired at the monster, but the exiled king told local townspeople of the encounter. Like so many elements of the Jersey Devil story, no contemporary historical documentation can be found to substantiate this incident. Commodore Stephen Decatur, the American naval hero, also became connected with the legend when he supposedly encountered the creature while inspecting the forging of cannonballs at Hanover Mills Iron Works in the Pine Barrens in the early nineteenth century. Subsequent embellished accounts claimed that Decatur had fired a cannon at the creature, but missed, as it darted by him and flew away. To date, no reliable primary source exists to show that this event occurred. Despite this, the story still gets repeated.[34] Therefore, the two most famous people who allegedly encountered the Jersey Devil left no letters or diaries detailing their experiences. It seems unlikely that they would have made no note of such a highly unusual experience.[35] From all regions of New Jersey and eastern Pennsylvania, hundreds of people claimed to see the creature. Descriptions varied greatly, from a galloping animal with horseshoes on its feet to a flying monster resembling a large Sandhill Crane, which actually did once live in the New Jersey pinelands.

When a councilman in Trenton saw the Jersey Devil the panic intensified.[36] Another posse of armed men formed, but it neither found nor captured the monster. The posse looked in the deepest woods as entire towns were put on curfew. The scant evidence produced usually consisted of hoofprints in the mud or snow, likely made by horses. These hoofprints were reproduced in newspaper illustrations as proof that the monster was still around. Some illustrations revealed iron horseshoes on the creature. A few people undoubtedly wondered how the Jersey Devil had managed to have its metal horseshoes made and fitted.

The capture of a Jersey Devil by the Ninth and Arch Street Dime Museum–sponsored hunt was not the last time such a claim would be asserted. In 1911 a Philadelphia goldfish breeder claimed he had found a live devil in his aquarium. Being only two inches long, it did not impress. As is typical in such cases, the report did not say what eventually happened to the diminutive creature.[37] Another capture story came along a year later. A pair of fishermen working off the coast of Brigantine, New Jersey, claimed they had battled a five-foot-long monster as they collected shad in their nets. They managed to get the feisty thing aboard and brought it back to shore, where a crowd gathered to gawk at it. With its physical strength and rows of menacing teeth, it seemed, they said, a cross between an alligator and the Jersey Devil, "which several years ago gave the entire Eastern states a fright."[38] In 1920, fishermen off the South Jersey coast, not far from Leeds Point, claimed they too had battled a bizarre Jersey Devil–like creature with "eight flexible arms like those of an octopus."[39]

When it wasn't accosting fishermen, the Jersey Devil augmented its diet by stealing chickens. In August 1919 a woman named Lena Bergeson claimed to have caught a Jersey Devil in her chicken coop. She went after it with a pitchfork and stabbed it several times. When a neighbor arrived on the scene, he too pinned the "What-is-it" with a pitchfork. The pair then beat the hapless creature with clubs until dead. They said it had the head of a squirrel, a body the size of a large dog, and looked like a possum. Having dispatched the beast they went off looking for its "lair."[40] A year later another "chicken killer" story appeared. A farmer claimed the "What-is-it?" had eaten his poultry, as well. It had a "head like a pig and eyes like a parrot . . . with a tail like a squirrel." The farmer captured it in a trap.[41] Despite the claims of these various stories, no follow-up was ever made. The story appeared and then disappeared. The danger of such reports is that later enthusiasts, not understanding the spurious, satirical, and exploitative nature of the stories, take them at face value.

Once established, the Jersey Devil legend began to grow in ways few would have anticipated. The name had acquired a life of its own well before it graced a professional hockey team. In 1915 a "half-witted youth" from Philadelphia had already acquired it as a nickname. A street kid pulling small-time break-ins (including a candy store) came to be known as "The Jersey Devil."[42] Later, during his none too brilliant career, Philadelphia boxer Johnny Russell used the nickname "Unk" as well as "Jersey Devil."[43]

The 1950s brought about a renewed interest in the legend. One popular sighting at Whitesbog, in the Pine Barrens, was later found to be a hoax: someone had used a bear's foot to make false tracks in the sand. Then, in 1957, a massive forest fire raged through the Wharton State Forest. After it had been extinguished, newspapers ran the photograph of a strange animal carcass, which some claimed was the Jersey Devil. It was found near Hampton Furnace by a forester with the then state Department of Conservation, but no study of the remains could conclusively identify it. No written report on it was ever issued. Therefore, there is no reason to believe this was anything other than a hoax. Local authorities were so convinced it was a fake that, in order to keep the curious from flooding the area in 1957, Greenwich Township police put up signs saying: "The Jersey Devil is a hoax."[44]

Monster sightings continued through the 1960s, with local or state police investigating some of the cases. One, in particular, is interesting. A farmer named Steven Silkotch reported to the State Police that "some animal" killed a large number of his ducks, several geese, six cats and dogs, including a ninety-pound German shepherd.[45] Logic suggests this was not a "deer-like flying creature," as the Jersey Devil is frequently described, but rather a large predator, such as a bear, although bear sightings were rare at that time in that part of New Jersey. The State Police were unable to take a plaster cast of the large paw prints found due to the rain-soaked soil. In the 1960s a Camden group put up a $10,000 reward for the creature's capture. The Hunt Brother's Circus then upped the ante, offering $100,000 for it. Their plan included putting it on display and making what they hoped would be a fortune off of it.[46]

Reports of strange doings in the pines and even in New Jersey's small towns and cities continued to feature the Jersey Devil. It seems that once a local story of an alleged sighting had taken root, other people began to see, and even search for, the creature. Virtually all of the "sightings" were embellished with nonsensical details. The monster's description had settled into a routine: an overall kangaroo-like appearance, a deer-like body, or the body of an impala or panther. Others called it bear-like, or, as it appeared in the Larner Diary, it was reported to be "as large as a moose with leather wings."[47] In a sighting in Burlington in 1909 a citizen described it as "three and a half feet high, with a head like a collie dog and a face like a horse."[48]

Meanwhile, the stories of sightings by Pine Barrens campers, and even city dwellers, increased. Anything strange or inexplicable was labeled the work of the Jersey Devil. The creature was "seen" on rooftops, flying in front of horse-drawn wagons, running in circles around houses, racing down cobblestone streets, and in the darkness surrounding campsites. It was, in effect, achieving fame beyond a typical local legend. As Watson Buck, a longtime resident of New Jersey's pines, said: "People 'round here say they don't believe such nonsense, but they don't say disbelieve it." He went on to say, "Form your own opinion."[49]

More recently, some people have claimed to have seen the Jersey Devil fly over their car while they were on the Garden State Parkway or on one of the lonely sandy roads in the pines. Jersey Devil search organizations have mounted expeditions to look for the creature. A national network television show also featured footage showing something large flying in the sky at dusk. Thus popular speculation continued, despite the complete lack of hard, indisputable evidence. As a friend of ours recently quipped, if there was a Jersey Devil in the pinelands it surely would have been run over by now by a tour bus roaring along the Garden State Parkway en route to Atlantic City. Something missing from previous attempts to find the Jersey Devil was an underlying theory to explain its existence, some way of making such a creature seem plausible. By the latter part of the twentieth century a new philosophy of monster enthusiasm answered the call.

Cryptozoology

The renewed interest in the Jersey Devil in the 1950s and '60s came about in part as a result of the explosion of interest in the new field of cryptozoology (the search for mythical creatures as living entities). Headlines about the Loch Ness Monster, the Abominable Snowman, and Bigfoot brought monsters to the forefront of the public imagination. Newspaper headlines around the world, as well as the popular men's adventure magazines of the day, bulged with stories about encounters with sea monsters and anomalous primates. Interest in monsters seemed new, but it had a long history.

Scholars began looking for and trying to explain monstrous creatures as far back as antiquity. Discussions in Pliny's *Natural History*, Ovid's *Metamorphoses*, and Lucretius's *On the Nature of Things*, just to name a few, helped establish the pursuit of monstrous creatures as a legitimate exercise. Monsters could be used as vehicles to study various intellectual topics. As a result of their investigations, early naturalists often came to one of several conclusions about monsters: legends referred to animals not widely known, but confused for monsters; the creatures actually did exist; or they originated in the imagination.

The historical search for monsters often revealed unexpected realities about the natural world. Monster hunters learned about the physical environments of the creatures they pursued. When the monster turned out to be an animal they did not know, they learned its habits, lifestyle, and mating rituals. When a legend proved spurious, investigators could still gain insights into the cultures that created them. They also learned about human nature. In their efforts to understand werewolves, Early Modern period authors began to argue that lycanthropy was a mental disorder, not magical shapeshifting. Authors such as Ulisse Aldrovandi, Fortunio Liceti, and even Carl Linneaus used the study of monstrous creatures to work out the diversity of life on earth. Their work allowed for ways to differentiate between the biologically plausible and the outright nonsensical.

In 1699 the pioneering English comparative anatomist Edward Tyson (1651–1708) showed that primates were not monsters, but genuine, separate species related to humans. He did this by doing the first medical dissection of an actual primate and then publishing his work, accompanied by meticulously accurate illustrations of a bonobo's musculature and anatomy. By extension, Tyson also helped demolish the long-held myth of the cynocephali (the dog-headed men) by showing that primates like the baboon only looked vaguely like humans, but were not actually human, as was thought during the Middle Ages. In the nineteenth century, Richard Owen argued that sea-monster reports came from observers misconstruing marine life they little understood. His work showed that what was thought to be sightings of mythical creatures was actually evidence of how whales copulated. When Charles Darwin articulated the idea of natural selection he used monstrosity to learn about the process of heredity. The pursuit of monsters throughout the nineteenth century helped prove the dubious nature of many monsters and also helped explain questions of generation, the spread of disease, and evolution.

For naturalists such as Conrad Gesner (1516–65) and Ulisse Aldrovandi (1522–1605), the study of monsters, wonders, and novelties did not undermine their worldviews, but caused them to modify their thinking in order to make their cosmologies whole and rational. If monsters were real, they had to be accounted for. This is an important context for modern researchers to understand. Monsters helped bridge the gap between the learned and the lay population. Intellectual distance could be surmounted because the public's appetite for monsters was as powerful as that of scholars. As a result, both impressive learned tomes and cheaply made pamphlets and broadsides on monsters rolled off printing presses, to be snatched up by a wide reading public.

Ulisse Aldrovandi's grand epic, *Monstrorum Historia* (1642), follows the model of a traditional cabinet of curiosities, starting with undeformed man at the top of the universal chain of being. There follows a rogue's gallery of monstrous races: humans with huge ears that trail to the ground (*Homo fanesius auritus*); others with huge lips or four eyes parade by. It then moves on to conventional monstrous births: what are today called birth defects. Rendered in striking detail, individuals with multiple arms and heads or no arms or no legs and conjoined twins of several types appear, including one of a man and a wolf man similar to the cynocephali.

The scholarly engagement with monsters of all types permeates the history of biology and natural history, and contributed in subtle but important ways to biological systemization, classification, and evolutionary studies.

While they did not all share the same motivations and intentions, one of the great meta-projects of natural historians has always been to take nature and organize it in an understandable and rational system. Whether trying simply to arrange plants and animals on a list, show diverse creation, or explain evolution, many natural philosophers were confronted and confounded by the need to account for monsters. If real, these creatures had to fit into the wider scheme of life. Carl Linnaeus, Richard Owen, and other influential scientists all studied and pondered monsters. Whether sea serpents, sciopods, cynocephali, werewolves, or Bigfoot, monsters found themselves either embraced, shoehorned into the great chain of being, or ignominiously expelled. Regardless of how they were treated, this engagement with monstrous creatures helped pave the way for the modern understanding of biology.

As science largely turned away from monsters, amateurs with a taste for the strange and unusual embraced cryptozoology as their own domain. All science practitioners until the seventeenth century can be classified as amateurs: they did not receive pay for their work, and few had formal training in the sciences. They did their work for the love of it rather than as an official job or out of the need to earn a living. That began to change when individuals such as Robert Hooke (1635–1703), of the Royal Society, began to find employment as instructors and demonstrators of science. By the later nineteenth century, job opportunities for a wide range of science practitioners had opened up in academia and in the corporate and government worlds. This led to a widening gap between the new professionals and their counterparts of the older, amateur tradition. This also led to a shift in power and control of science away from the amateurs and firmly into the hands of professionals. The struggles and relationships between these groups became an engine driving modern science. The professional/amateur tension is an important aspect of the history of science.

The mainstream investigation into monsters began to end in the later nineteenth century, spurred on by the work of the English naturalist Richard Owen. One of the best known biologists of his day, Owen (1804–92) had a particular interest in large "monstrous" creatures. In the 1830s he coined the name *dinosauria* to describe the large reptile-like creatures then just being discovered. Owen, because of his political connections and scientific celebrity, regularly received reports of sea serpents from the British Admiralty. Owen commented, both privately and publically, on the infamous HMS *Daedalus* incident. When a British warship captain and several of his officers made public statements that they had encountered a large snake-like monster as they passed the Cape of Good Hope in 1848, the press went wild. When Owen said that the crew, despite their honor, had misidentified a large

The most famous sea-monster sighting of the nineteenth century. The HMS *Daedalus* encounters a strange creature during her 1848 cruise.

sea lion, a good bit of the wind went out of the story's sails. His detailed analysis of several of the most prominent sea monster sightings of the day led Owen to conclude that observers, who had little or no experience with such creatures, often misidentified whales and other large marine creatures. Mainstream science began to back away from monster studies altogether.[50] Added to this, advances in Darwinian evolutionary biology, hereditary studies, and direct examination of monster legends by scholars ended the widespread interest in monstrous creatures by the growing professional class of intellectuals.

The last scientist of the nineteenth century to tackle the question of monsters, Dutch zoologist A. C. Oudemans (1858–1943), did an extensive study of sea monster sightings. His book, *The Great Sea Serpent* (1892), went virtually unnoticed by his professional colleagues. Rediscovered in the 1950s and '60s, Oudemans's work influenced an entire generation of amateur investigators. The end of scientific interest in monstrous creatures left a vacuum that opened the way for the emergence of cryptozoology.

Two professional science practitioners stepped into that vacuum and kept interest in monsters alive for amateurs. The Belgian zoologist Bernard Heuvelmans (1916–2001) and the Cambridge-trained biologist Ivan Sanderson (1911–73) became the point men for the new wave in monster enthusiasm.

I. Monſtrum alatum, & cornutum inſtar
Cacodæmonis.

A very Jersey Devil–like creature, Monstrum alatum, from Ulisse Aldrovandi, *Monstrorum Historia* (Nicolai Tebaldine, 1642). This image can also be found in Gaspar Schott's *Physica Curiosa* (1697).

Unlike the first searchers for the Loch Ness Monster in the 1930s, Heuvelmans and Sanderson had formal science training. Following their books *On the Track of Unknown Animals* (1958) and *Abominable Snowmen: Legend Come to Life* (1961), respectively, Heuvelmans and Sanderson inspired legions of amateur monster enthusiasts ready to follow their precepts as Oudemans had inspired them.

The 1950s and '60s were a Golden Age of cryptozoology. During this period the Yeti, or Abominable Snowman, in Central Asia and the Sasquatch, or Bigfoot, in North America drew worldwide attention. Renewed interest came in the form of the Patterson film. Shot by a pair of Bigfoot hunters, Roger Patterson and Robert Gimlin, the film showed what looked like a Bigfoot walking through the woods of Northern California on October 20, 1967. Though less than a minute long, jumpy and grainy, the film caused a sensation (its authenticity is still debated). Along with the Patterson film, large, anomalous footprints also started to appear in the wooded regions of

America and Canada. Aspiring monster hunters across the country headed out into the nearest woods hoping to come across such a creature.

Some mainstream scientists began to reconsider cryptozoology as a legitimate enterprise worth their attention. Most notable amongst these was Gordon "Grover" Sanders Krantz (1931–2002).[51] A university-trained paleoanthropologist, Krantz became fascinated by the reports of giant ape-like creatures that were beginning to get public notice in the western United States and Canada. His training in human and primate locomotion suggested to him that not all these reports of hairy bipedal beasts could be hoaxes. Delving into the material and collecting casts of purported Sasquatch footprints convinced him that these creatures were real. He began publishing books and articles based upon his researches. His appearance in the media, most notably as a guest on the popular television programs *In Search of . . .* and *Arthur C. Clarke's Mysterious World* in the 1980s, created excitement, and his status as a professor at Washington State University lent credibility to monster hunting. Renewed fascination with monsters extended to the Jersey Devil as well.

The world of cryptozoology came to the Jersey Devil slowly. Early authors on the topic, such as W. F. Mayer in the nineteenth century and Francis Bazley Lee and Henry Charlton Beck in the twentieth, saw the Jersey Devil legend as simply that: a strange tale of macabre goings-on in dark, forbidding forests and having little basis in reality. The WPA Guide of 1939 saw it as an outright joke. Taking their cue from Sanderson, Heuvelmans, and the philosophy of cryptozoology, modern Jersey Devil enthusiasts still saw the story as one about a bizarre human-dragon hybrid, but they approached it as a genuine biological entity, which could be found, photographed, and even captured. It is easy to understand the lure of monster hunting in general and Jersey Devil hunting in particular.

The Jersey Devil's home is an ideal landscape in which to chase a monster. Trekking through the Pine Barrens on a summer's day with cicadas rattling and hawks screeching overhead, or in winter as snow falls upon the trees, makes for an enchanting romantic experience. In the depths of the forest, time itself seems to lose meaning. At night the darkness is so deep one can conjure up many frightening creatures lurking behind every tree. One almost expects to come around a corner and encounter a colonial era farmhouse, with its Quaker inhabitants going about their business, smiling a welcome as you approach, or to hear the fluttering of large leathery wings.

The minor frenzy that had bubbled up in the 1950s over Jersey Devil sightings had died down again by the late 1970s. Jersey Devil studies were invigorated by the publication of McCloy and Miller's *The Jersey Devil* (1978). The book was full of fantastic stories and had no irksome footnotes, citations, or other historical/scholarly baggage to get in the way of the fun. McCloy and Miller never came to a conclusion as to whether the Jersey Devil was a real animal or a figure of mythology. There is no mention of Daniel Leeds: the authors merely state that the legend goes back to the colonial era. They present a new monster ripe for the chase. If you hailed from the East Coast and wanted to hunt monsters and could not get out to California or Washington to search for Bigfoot, the Pine Barrens was an easy car ride away. As an aspiring monster hunter, one could get in on the ground floor and perhaps be the one to produce his or her own Patterson film—or even a body part or two.

Unlike monster hunters of old, content with pursuing their prey across texts, cryptozoologists adopted a more adventurous approach. Jersey Devil aficionados regularly head into the Pine Barrens on expeditions to find the creature they think prowls those dark precincts. As of this writing there are at least three organized groups, along with many individuals and loose affiliations that actively search for the monster. The Monmouth County Parks System even sponsors tongue-in-cheek Jersey Devil hunts on Halloween for children. Believers argue over the minutiae of physical evidence, such as tracks in the snow, and compile lists of sightings by famous people in order to prove that the creature is, in fact, a flesh and blood animal.[52] Unfortunately for cryptozoologists, no physical evidence for the Jersey Devil exists except for the supposed remains of a creature discovered after the forest fire of 1957. There are only scattered, inconsistent reports about its behavior. Its reputed morphology flies in the face of any reasonable evolutionary biology; thus it resists labeling as a genuine cryptid.[53] Nevertheless, some cryptozoologists have suggested that the creature may be similar to a long-extinct *Tarsus Pterodactyl*, though that remains an obviously speculative idea.[54]

By the 1990s the availability of infrared night vision devices and trail cameras opened new avenues for tracking elusive creatures. However, few of the Jersey Devil hunters brought with them the historical knowledge of how the myth began or experience searching through history to see how such a creature could have been born, and most importantly, that the Jersey Devil did not exist in a vacuum.

CHAPTER SIX

The Devil Becomes a Star

WHEN LOOKING INTO LEGENDS one must avoid simply parroting information from websites, blogs, and other dubious sources of the paranormal "echo chamber," without confirming the veracity of such information.[1] Proper historical techniques and primary text analysis can expose the origins of monster legends and show how they fit into a wider context. Very few of the Jersey Devil aficionados who chased the creature in the twentieth and twenty-first centuries followed this advice. Their persistence in trying to find a flesh and blood animal did nothing to make the creature real; it did, however, make it a star.

The Jersey Devil can be found, not in the forest, but in the library—in particular, in publications of the period. Almanacs were the pop culture publishing of the seventeenth and eighteenth centuries. Cheaply produced and sold, they provided a calendar year with the phases of the moon, sunrise and sunset, the change of seasons, and other information pertinent to the farming communities that made up the bulk of the early American population. Weather forecasting was an important part of almanac publishing. These charts followed widely held notions of astrology, accounting for the weather as well as the movements of the heavens. They utilized mathematics and astronomical information to predict eclipses. In addition, almanacs also contained local news, church meeting schedules, political musings, and even the occasional humorous anecdote. If the almanac compiler felt so inclined, he could give free rein to his intellectual proclivities or pander to his readers' base instincts. It was not unusual for a compiler to mention the birth of a monster. This proved so popular that publishers began to produce works focused exclusively upon monsters.

Often accompanied by crude but lurid woodblock illustrations, these booklets looked much like almanacs, but without the yearly calendar. They often focused upon one particular monstrous birth, describing how it came about and how it affected the local community. When such an event occurred it would draw much attention, especially if some catastrophe or other community disaster could be associated with it. The illustrations of such creatures would be made based upon descriptions by eyewitnesses. The artists themselves rarely saw the subject of their drawings with their own eyes.

As a result, the drawings accentuated the bizarre, but rarely resembled the actual birth.

A typical example of a pamphlet on an animal monster is "Some Account of a Sheep, Shewed Alive to the Royal Society" (1754). This particular sheep was born with a horn growing out of its neck. Members of London's Royal Society (the first science society developed in the West) marveled at the creature's anatomy.[2] Such works sold well; an illiterate person could look at the illustrations even if they could not read the words. The spread of monster lore also came in the form of full-sized books.

A popular text first published shortly after Daniel Leeds arrived in the New World also contributed to the popularity of monsters. The anonymous work known as *Aristotle's Masterpiece* (1684) was an early medical book on gynecology. Cobbled together from several previous works (not from anything Aristotle ever wrote), the book is a basic home primer on birth and other topics related to midwifery. It went through many editions in England and eventually in America. Though covering many aspects of the birthing process—and notoriously seen as a sex manual—the illustrations that accompanied the text showed monstrous human births. These illustrations, at their best crudely done, fit the sensibility of the age. The publishers of *Aristotle's Masterpiece* knew how much the reading public enjoyed such monstrous images and knew that their inclusion would boost sales. They also allowed the curious to read the book under the guise of learning science and medicine.[3] In some versions, the text included an illustration that looks surprisingly similar to popular ideas of what the Jersey Devil looked like.

Such pictures appeared regularly as cover illustrations meant to entice almanac readers. In the 1760s John Mein created *Bickerstaff's Boston Almanac*. Mein had a penchant for the weird and regularly graced the covers of his almanac with illustrations of giants and other wonders. In 1785 he used a crude copy of Edward Tyson's drawing of the bonobo with a walking stick. This may be the first time the image of a primate appeared in a North American publication.[4]

The monsters appearing in American almanacs and books had ancestors. While monsters populated medieval manuscripts in profusion, they also leapt to the pages of printed matter. Woodblock and movable-type printing was established in Europe by the 1450s and made monsters even more popular. They would get their widest exposure through the spread of pamphlets and tracts that were produced quickly, cheaply, and in some numbers. The subject of monsters came in two categories: mythical beasts and monstrous births of animals, especially humans.

One of the more popular monsters depicted during the Early Modern

Original in the John Carter Brown Library at Brown University

The publishers of *Bickerstaff's Almanac* had an interest in the weird and wonderful and often included drawings of strange creatures, both human and animal, on the cover.

period, the Monk Calf, first appeared in a pamphlet by Martin Luther and Philip Melanchthon. *The Papal Ass of Rome and the Monk Calf of Freyberg* (1523) included an illustration of the purported creature as a pig-like bipedal beast with layers of flesh hanging from its body. It fitted the anti-Catholic diatribes and prurient rumormongering meant to win converts to the Protestant cause by turning them away from the establishment. The skin of the Monk Calf mimicked the religious garb of a Catholic monk. Luther used the creature as a metaphor for the Church and the displeasure the Church caused God. "Monsters," Luther and Melanchthon said, "most times doe note and demonstrate unto us the ire and wrath of God."[5] Monks were accused by anti-Catholics of trying to achieve godliness through special clothing instead of genuine spirituality. Monks' lives, Luther claimed, "consist of nothing but gobbling food, of drinking, and of sex."[6] Thus, they were not true religionists, but ghastly imposters, just like this malformed monstrosity. The Monk Calf was, Luther said, God's way of producing a sign to warn people of the perfidy of heretics.

Martin Luther's pamphlet proved a popular model for later authors who used monsters as hammers against the Catholic Church and monarchy in general, and to remind readers of God's ever-present power. The more rabid tracts, like Luther's, saw the Church and its functionaries— priests, bishops, and naturally, the pope—as monsters. These authors had little interest in natural history. The creatures depicted in these pamphlets could sometimes be outrageous concoctions, along with the usual two-headed babies or deformed pigs. Luther's Monk Calf was only the most widely known and copied.

Such monster tracts showed the wrath God would bring down, not only on kings and countries, but on commoners as well. These can be collectively known as scare tracts. The author of *A Declaration of a Strange and Wonderful Monster* (1645), for example, saw one particular creature as "a wonderful manifestation of God's anger against wicked and profane people." The Protestant mother in the story had given birth to a monstrous child, the author claimed, because God had damned her for marrying a Papist (Catholic). Her poor choice of husbands brought on this terrible calamity. Other Protestant women should, therefore, be careful of whom they pick to father their children.

A pamphlet of 1652 on the birth of a deformed pig said, "these strange and monstrous things which Almighty God sendeth amongst us that we would not be frightened of his Almighty power." In another, a child born in Verona supposedly grew so rapidly it achieved the size of an adult in just a few months. This "child" then began to spout prophesies about the downfall of various countries, including France and Poland. "The Inquisition," the author states, "has since taken the child into their custody." Nonhuman monsters appeared in these pamphlets as well. In *A Certaine Relation of a Hog-Faced Woman* (1640), *Great News from Saxony or a New and Strange Relation of the Mighty Giant Koorbmep* (1680), and *A Most Strange but True Account of Very Large Sea-Monster* (1704), theologians and other self-appointed moralists felt obliged to remind their audiences—of mostly poor and barely literate peasants and working-class people—that God watched them in their little affairs and would bring down swift and terrible judgment on them in the form of a monster. Only rarely did the monster pamphleteers single out a noble or wealthy family. It was the lower classes who were most prone to producing monsters.

The wake of the Protestant Reformation produced an increase in not only

A Declaration of a Strange and Wonderfull Monster (1646). This pamphlet is typical of the publications pandering to the widespread popular interest in monsters. Such works helped pave the way for the appearance of the Leeds Devil.

popular, sensational pamphlets in the style of Luther's but also more scholarly tomes. Some of these, including Conrad Lycosthenes's *Prodigiorum ac Ostentorum Chronicum* (1557) and Pierre Boaistuau's *Histoires Prodigieuses* (1559), continued the trend of monsters as omens or of the perfidy of the Catholic Church, but they leaned more in the biological direction. More interested in natural history than in scolding the Church was Guillaume Rondelet's *Libri de Piscibus Merinis* (1554), and then Ambroise Paré's *Des Monstres* (1573). Whether meant to skewer the Church or elucidate the reality of wondrous creatures, these books brought monster studies to a wider audience than ever. As time went by, however, the view that monsters represented portents of evil times or God's wrath, like a comet or an earthquake, went out of fashion in all but the most popular and sensationalist forms of

books and broadsides. Renaissance-era humanist naturalist monster enthusiasts and collectors of curiosities of various stripes in Europe and Tudor England still relied upon Greco-Roman sources, combining them with Christian morality, but they increasingly viewed animals and monsters as topics of
biological wonder instead of God's wrath.[7]

Two groups took scientific interest in monsters. Physicians and naturalist
collectors saw monsters as vehicles to understand the natural world. The
general notion included the idea that abnormalities and unusual body shapes
could be used to study things like generation and the general order of nature. While individual members of these two groups still found a theological
component in the meaning of monsters, they worked to see a more naturalistic and scientific view of these entities as well. This interest spurred them
on to examine the biological underpinning of life. As monsters were so different, it was thought their differences could shed light on the process of life.
Through this interest in the mechanics of procreation and heredity, biological diversity and systemization would be better understood, as would questions of transmutation. The seventeenth century also saw the spread of Ba-
conian experimental philosophy and empiricism, with its emphasis on direct
observation and study of the type that Daniel and Titan Leeds had embraced:
an approach that would bring monster studies to new heights of rigor, but
ultimately undermine them.

Doctors of the Monstrous

Naturalists comprised the largest group of monster enthusiasts during the
Renaissance. However, physicians and surgeons also took notice of how monsters, particularly monstrous births, influenced human generation and reproduction. While a number of texts appeared from medical men who included discussions of monstrous births—especially works on gynecology and
midwifery—two stand out during this period. Jacob Rueff (1500–58) worked
as city physician at Zurich and instructed midwives, though he considered
women lesser versions of men. His *De Conceptu et Generatione Hominis* (1554),
aimed at physicians, surgeons, and particularly midwives, covered the techniques of childbirth. As with so many authors of books on obstetrics and
gynecology, Rueff saw monstrous births as fascinating subjects that could
bring insight into generation and heredity and were an easy way to attract
nonspecialist readers.[8] (Books on childbirth, such as the wildly popular
Aristotle's Masterpiece, which still saw print into the nineteenth century, continued to carry illustrations of monstrous births, when virtually nothing else
from the text had accompanying pictures, as a way of increasing sales.) Rueff
based his book in part upon Andreas Vesalius's *De Humani Corporis Fabrica*

(1543) and Conrad Gesner's *Historiae Animalium* (1551–58), as well as an earlier obstetrics book *Der Swengeren Fruwen und Hebammen Rosengarten* (1508). He subscribed to the divine origin of monsters when he described one particular deformity as having originated in God's displeasure with sodomy.[9]

Another important author on obstetrics and monsters was the Frenchman Ambroise Paré. While the story of his early life is a bit muddled, Paré (1510–90) began his career as an apprentice barber-surgeon. He then joined the French army as a field surgeon and saw extensive battlefield service in a number of the many religious wars that ravaged Europe during the Reformation. Amid the blood and death of combat he saw how useless the traditional employment of hot oil and cauterization for sword and gunshot wounds and amputations was. He developed an alternative method, which abandoned cauterization in favor of surgically tying off arteries to stop blood flow. His method proved exceptionally successful, and the survival rate of wounded soldiers under his care improved. He rose steadily up the ranks of French medicine by making a number of choice associations and friendships.[10] He eventually became chief surgeon to Henri III and counted the political philosopher Montaigne a friend.[11]

Along with surgical techniques, Paré pioneered the design and implementation of mechanical prosthetics for amputees. Paré wrote on obstetrics and gynecology and helped develop techniques for inducing labor without drugs. He believed birth defects such as clubfoot resulted from the mother sitting in an odd position or being injured. These would then be transferred to the fetus in utero. He seems a paragon of the increasingly influential new secular science and experimental philosophy. However, Paré is a fascinating example of the border regions between theology and science which was a hallmark of this age. While his actual religious affiliations and sympathy—between Catholicism and Protestantism—are debated by scholars today, he lived and wrote as a deeply religious man. He famously said that he treated his patients, but God cured them. He felt doctors could only cure natural ailments, not supernatural ones caused by sorcerers or demons.[12]

Like Rueff, Paré wanted average people, even women, to know of medical procedures and the techniques of birthing. This attitude did not endear him to the Paris medical establishment. His monster work—which at the time was thought of by some as an unimportant and needless distraction from proper medical issues—also did not impress his colleagues. Historian A. W. Bates argues that Paré included this material in his text as a way of boosting sales of his book outside the medical community.[13]

Paré's interest in monsters stemmed from his curiosity about human generation, but also a general interest with the outré. He once claimed to have encountered a Toad-in-the-Hole. An unverified phenomenon—which still has proponents today—Toad-in-the-Hole events occur when seemingly solid stones are broken open to reveal a fully formed toad or frog alive inside. Paré's encounter with just such a specimen led him to think about spontaneous generation and how monster studies might bring some insight into how living things could appear without any apparent procreation being involved.[14]

Paré began working on his magnum monster opus, *Des Monstres et Prodiges,* in 1570 as a way of gaining a better understanding of human reproduction. He wanted to understand what caused the abnormal instead of the normal. "Monsters," he said, "are things that appear outside the course of nature" while "wonders" went against nature.[15] He argued that God allowed for the deviation, yet there were natural reasons why deformities came about. He was unwilling to simply fob off monstrosity on God completely. He began the book by articulating thirteen reasons monsters appeared. First and foremost monsters indicated God's glory or his wrath. This, however, accounted for only a few instances. The majority of monsters, such as babies with more than one head or set of limbs, appeared as a result of either too much or too little "seed." They could be caused by some physical problem with the mother's reproductive system or an injury to the mother during pregnancy that might cause a deformed skull. He added finally that they could be caused by the machinations of "demons and devils" and "wicked spital beggars." Despite his references to the supernatural, Paré worked to establish a more naturalistic set of understandings and explanations. He included representations of monsters, including the Monk Calf, as ways of explaining their origins in biological terms. Paré extended his discussion of monstrous creatures to his work on surgery as well. In *Opera Chirurgica* (1594), along with drawings and discussions of mechanical hands and legs, Paré presented the image of a griffin-like creature, the Succanth, as a possible variation on a monstrous birth.

Increasingly, authors like Paré began to reject the religious and political trappings of monster studies and stuck to scientific and prosaic explanations and examinations. Being of his time, he could not quite let go of all the old ways.[16] Guillaume Rondelet's *Libri de Piscabus Marinis* (1554–55) included his direct observations of fish and other aquatic life, yet also made reference to Luther's Monk Calf to explain abnormalities. Despite his apparent "scientific" approach, Paré wrote in the popular tradition of wonders and religious pamphleteers. In describing a monster that came out of a chicken egg in the home of a barrister in March 1569, Paré said, "The present monster you see depicted here was found inside an egg." Like some erudite carnival barker, Paré goes on to say that it had "the face and visage of a man, his hair made up of little snakes." Then, for real impact, he finished by exclaiming that the monstrosity was "completely alive."[17] In leaning toward a less theological stance on monsters some authors still clung—unconsciously or not—to the superstitions of the day.

The monster writers of the sixteenth century, whether physician or naturalist (many were both), followed a pattern of organization for their books. They described the animal and then told stories about it whose structure was often taken from mythology and ancient texts. Frenchman Pierre Belon (1517–64) eschewed the tradition of natural history, writing by using drawings of animal skeletons to illustrate his work in addition to the drawings of the live creatures. In the 1550s he employed a comparative anatomy approach: something all but unknown to his contemporary virtuosi and collectors. His books on fishes, birds, and mammals pointed out the similarities between species. He included one of the first drawings of a human and a bird skeleton positioned side by side. Like Jacob Rueff, he took inspiration from Vesalius's influential book on human anatomy, *De Humani Corporus Fabrica* (1543), which featured exacting renderings of human anatomy.[18] Belon worked to turn the approach Vesalius had employed with human anatomy to animal structure. While Belon stood apart from his contemporaries, a few authors held an especially influential place in monster studies.

End of an Era

A major thread in the origin of the Jersey Devil springs from this history of monstrous births. The Leeds Devil legend, some argue, began as a genuine monstrous birth attributed to Mother Leeds, but it may have been influenced by the monstrous births of the Puritan heretics Anne Hutchinson and Mary Dyer of the 1630s. Regardless of which actual monstrous birth, or none, served as a rough template for the Leeds Devil, to turn such a baffling, even horrifying event into a monster story would not have been an unusual thing. Despite the advances in medical explanations of birth defects, some still reacted by interpreting them as supernatural, as in the cases of Hutchinson and Dyer. Efforts were being made by philosophers to understand such seemingly irrational incidents.

The last of the great monster collectors in the virtuoso tradition of the Early Modern period was the Italian Fortunio Liceti (1577–1657). Holding a doctorate in philosophy and a medical degree, Liceti's *De monstrorum natura, caussis, et differentiis libri duo* (1616) dealt with biological malformation at the embryonic level.[19] This book appeared just before English settlers

Jersey Devil–like creatures from Ulisse Aldrovandi, *Monstrorum Historia* (Nicolai Tebaldine, 1642). This image can also be found in Gaspar Schott's *Physica Curiosa* (1697). Monsters like these were very popular with scholars and the public alike. Publishers often reproduced them in many different books for the shock value.

began to arrive in the Jerseys and so would have been known to the more literate among them. Eschewing theological explanations, Liceti saw monstrous births of both animals and humans as natural. He tried to explain deformities through hereditary causes rather than divine or demonic ones. Liceti argued that while conjoined twins, for example, were a rare but natural phenomenon, human-hybrids were not. Deformities and monsters appeared, he argued, as a result of nature trying to work its way around some natural biological impediment. Liceti wondered about the nature of the word *monster*. Rather than *monstrum* as portent, he asked if it came from *monstrare*, 'to show.' He did not think deformities were curses from God or "errors" by nature, but were instead nature's attempt to adapt. A two-headed baby was thus the result of not enough material for two or too much for one.[20] Along with the text Liceti included a number of drawings of monstrous births. His depiction of a Cyclops baby (born with a single eye in its forehead) is thought to be the first ever published, based on an original drawing by none other than Leonardo da Vinci.[21] Liceti's bent toward biology and away from theology presaged work by others.

The seventeenth century saw Francis Bacon (1561–1626) articulate the modern scientific method, which rejected reliance upon past authorities. Interestingly, Bacon did not reject monster studies. He argued that scholars should engage with the types of monsters and biological wonders the curiosity collectors focused on. In the *New Organon* (1620), the book that had so inspired Daniel Leeds, Bacon also wondered about speciation. While he thought one species transmuting into another "would be very difficult," he thought it would be a much easier proposition to vary the characteristics within a type. Either way, to better understand the process by which transmutation could take place or how "errors" of nature were produced and explained, it was important for naturalists to study monsters of all kinds. Toward this end Bacon said, "we have to make a collection or particular natural history of all prodigies and monstrous births of nature; of everything in short that is in nature new, rare, and unusual." It had to be done in a rigorous and scholarly manner to get the best results. Superstition should be avoided, as should "natural magic and alchemy."[22]

In 1662 one of the last major monster compendiums appeared. Written by German Jesuit Gaspar Schott (1608–66), it repeated material already well known, and it contained little original work. The *Physica Curiosa Sive Mirabilia Naturae et Artis* included the *Gallus Monstrosus*, the bizarre rooster. With it appeared cutaway drawings of eggs with human heads, with snakelike appendages inside. Schott also included drawings of primates, along with a "satyri" (resembling Mr. Tumnus from Narnia), cynocephali, a human with an elephant's head, as well as various hairy men and women. In the monsterologist tradition, Schott took many of the illustrations he used from other authors, including Edward Topsell. Primarily an engineer who wrote on hydraulics, Schott was mentored by Anastasias Kircher and kept up with the latest advances in the growing scientific revolution, corresponding with Robert Boyle.

Despite their efforts to medicalize and naturalize monsters, the curiosity collectors (who loved stuffed and pickled animals, the stranger the better) and scientific virtuosi fought an uphill battle. As they published their increasingly scientific and scholarly work, authors like Gesner, Paré, Aldrovandi, and others had to share space with popular broadsheets and pamphlets pouring

off presses in some profusion. The sensational interest in monsters continued as the naturalists looked more scholarly. Cheap pamphlets and broadsheets showed no sign of giving way. If anything, the production of the popular publications on monsters grew more vigorous. More of these tabloid-style
works saw print, purchase, and perusal than the expensive, lavishly illustrated
science books.

All this interest in monsters in Early Modern Europe influenced readers
and political pundits in America. The birth of the Leeds Devil and its later
transformation into the Jersey Devil had a very long gestation period in Euro-
American culture. It underwent changes as different authors ascribed different definitions and meanings to it. While the monstrous birth pamphlets
were normally one-off productions—there were never follow-ups to any particular booklet—monsters like the Jersey Devil took on larger lives and even
the characteristics of literary characters. With all this history behind it, the
only thing that would be odd about the Jersey Devil would have been if it
hadn't been born. It also contributed to creating offspring of its own.

Modern Relatives

Just south of the Jersey Devil's stomping grounds lies the less well-known
haunt of the Snallygaster. Calling the South Mountain region of Frederick
County, Maryland, home, the Snallygaster has an anatomy similar to that
of the Jersey Devil. With an overall horse-like body, this creature also has
hooves, horns, a forked tail, and leathery bat-like wings. Some newspaper
accounts have described it as a primate. It too has been called a "Jabberwock." Along with its morphology, the narrative arc of the Snallygaster par-
allels that of the Jersey Devil. According to legend, the creature first appeared
in 1735 (the same year as the Jersey Devil). It has appeared less often than
its northern cousin. When it does appear, it flies around and engages in various monstery hijinks, though nothing too violent or genuinely creepy.[23]

Though supposedly reaching back to 1735, public interest in the Snallygaster also begins in 1909. Newspaper accounts have appeared across the
twentieth century only sporadically. The legend seems to have begun with
the work of amateur historian of the South Mountain region Madeleine
Vinton Dahlgren (1825–98). The wife of the noted Civil War Union ad-
miral and weapons designer John A. Dahlgren (1809–70), she wrote novels
about life in Washington, DC, and the folklore of Maryland, with an eye
toward the odd. The origin of the Snallygaster is likely apocryphal, as all
mentions of the myth date no earlier than the late nineteenth century and
appear nowhere but in the work of Mrs. Dahlgren.

The idea of horse-like demon monsters are not restricted to North America. Another creature with a vague similarity to the Jersey Devil comes in the form of the Popobawa of Africa. Stories about this far more sinister version of the Jersey Devil began to appear in the Pemba Island region of Tanzania near the Zanzibar archipelago in the mid-1990s. The name derives from the Swahili word for *bat wing*. While having the same basic body plan as the Jersey Devil, the Popobawa can also shape-shift. It is said to regularly attack humans with some violence, including sexual assault. The first sightings of the creature are associated with a political revolution on Pemba in 1965. Occasional sightings came in during the 1970s and '80s, culminating in the media reports of the mid-1990s. The myth has certain religious overtones not found in the Jersey Devil. Believers claim that a Popobawa attack can be held off if the victim recites passages from the Koran. Other Arab elements include a popular origin story concerning a sheik who called up the Popobawa in the form of a jinn to get revenge on an enemy but who lost control of the demon, which then went off to follow its own path. It has also been seen as a folkloric reaction to the Zanzibar slave trade.[24] The Jersey Devil lived not only in the snowy forests of the Atlantic Coast or the hot dry lands of Africa; a Jersey Devil–like creature migrated to film, television, and books as well.

The Devil in the Media

By the late twentieth and early twenty-first centuries the Jersey Devil had gone from the realm of local legend to pop culture icon. Its first major appearance as such came in the 1930s, when the state of New Jersey chose it as its "state demon." Years later it became the mascot of a professional hockey team. The team began in the 1970s as the Kansas City Scouts, but then moved to Denver, Colorado, to become the Colorado Rockies. In 1982 the team moved again, this time to New Jersey. A public vote was held to see what name the team would adopt, and the winner was *The Jersey Devils*. Taking its cue from the descriptions of the creature, the team logo is a stylized NJ with the letter forms taking on devil horns and a spikey tail.

In 1993 the popular television series *The X-Files* aired an episode called "The Jersey Devil" in which FBI agents Mulder and Scully travel to Atlantic City to investigate the murders of several homeless people by a Bigfoot-like creature. They discover that some locals think the Jersey Devil is to blame. Mulder discovers that there is a male and female pair of hairy humanoids (he thinks they might be Neanderthals) at loose on the streets of the city that was, in part, founded by the Leeds family. The police kill both of these "Jersey Devils," but the final scene shows their offspring having escaped notice; they will presumably grow up to terrorize the streets as their parents did.

In a lighter vain, a 1995 episode of *Seinfeld* has Elaine Benes's boyfriend, David Puddy, inviting the gang to see a Jersey Devils versus New York Rangers game. Just before they leave to go to Madison Square Garden, Puddy shows up in a Devils uniform, his face painted like a devil. Shocked, Elaine questions whether she can date a "face painter." He shows great enthusiasm over the game, explaining, "Hey, I'm from Jersey, man!" His animation is such that, while screaming on the street "I'm the devil, I'm the devil!," he causes an innocent passing priest to have a heart attack.[25]

Television documentary programs about monsters, first beginning in the 1980s, found greater interest in the late 1990s and early twenty-first century. Series on the paranormal, such as *Monster Quest, Lost Tapes,* and *True Monsters,* all had episodes highlighting the Jersey Devil. It seemed that no self-respecting television series on monsters could do without segments on the flying dragon from the Pine Barrens. With this attention the Jersey Devil took its place in the pantheon of other famous cryptids, such as Bigfoot and the Loch Ness Monster.

New Jersey's most famous rock 'n' roll son, Bruce Springsteen, entered the fray for Halloween 2008, releasing the song "A Night with the Jersey Devil."[26] It is a fuzzy guitar blues number, supposedly intended to dissuade people from coming to his house trick-or-treating. While keeping the general outline of the story, he embellishes a bit. "Come back, kill six brothers and sisters," he growls, "kill poppa too, sway down momma, sway down low. They're gonna know me wherever I go!" A number of performers have created songs about the Jersey Devil available on YouTube, most in the country-blues style.

A number of movies using the Jersey Devil have been made. *The Barrens* (2012) and *Dark Was the Night* (2015) are typical of the genre. The plot lines usually involve people encountering the Jersey Devil in the forest. Unlike most actual sightings, where the creature does little, these story lines have it killing unsuspecting travelers and engaging in various forms of mayhem. When the victims try to tell the authorities, they are dismissed. At the end of *The Barrens* the protagonists, upset that the local police are not interested, head off into the woods. Like the posse of 1929, they intend for their expedition to find and then kill the creature.

The place one is most likely to find purported images of the Jersey Devil is YouTube. A number of short videos claiming to be footage of the actual creature can be found there. More elaborately produced documentaries about the legend—of varying levels of quality—also appear. Like so much footage of paranormal activity, the Jersey Devil videos are put forward as the product of unsuspecting videographers and innocent campers who "do not want their identities revealed" or who are of the "I didn't know this was on the tape until I watched it later" variety. None is particularly compelling or even mildly interesting.

There is at least one video game involving the Jersey Devil. PlayStation has a game geared toward a younger audience. The Devil is more of a bat here. The animated character battles an evil scientist who is creating human/vegetable hybrids. The Jersey Devil has also been used as a foil in a number of novels. Works by authors such as J. J. Crane (2014), Gary Botsch (2015), and Hunter Shea (2016) have used the devil as a plot device.

There are groups and individuals who go on expeditions into the woods to find the creature. These organizations can easily be found on the internet. Members of the group Jersey Devil Paranormal Investigations call themselves "truth seekers." They are joined by the Paranormal Society, Paranormal Investigation Group of New Jersey, and others who search for the elusive creature. They often host web forums and act as clearinghouses for video shot by others.

Conclusion

Once an obscure local legend, the tale of the Jersey Devil has become known worldwide. It has secured its place in modern pop culture and has become something of a social media darling. As an enduring myth, the Jersey Devil has served several purposes. From the days of Daniel and Titan Leeds, the story went from political insult to half-forgotten monster legend to a way to disparage people of the Pine Barrens to a case of mass hysteria caused by a publicity stunt. More recently it has become the quarry of paranormal investigators, the mascot of a professional hockey team, and the subject of television and movie production.

Myths often show this type of adaptability. While the Jersey Devil's morphology remained constant, its meaning changed over time. It managed to do this without ever uttering a single word. It will likely continue to evolve for each successive generation that investigates it. Ironically, however, few understood that all this began in the eighteenth century because an energetic, thoughtful man wanted to write an almanac and help improve the lives of his neighbors.

EPILOGUE

THE SNOW FELL GENTLY on the trees of the Pine Barrens as Daniel Leeds walked along the road leading to town from his house outside Burlington. In the distance he could just make out the bell tolling at St. Mary's church. As he walked, he contemplated his life. He could be proud of his accomplishments of publishing and political activism. His son Titan had also done well. Daniel Leeds did not know it, but several of his descendants would go on to success in farming and politics. History, however, would not be as kind to the Leeds family as he might have hoped. Accusations of political wrongdoing and occult activity resulted in their being turned into monsters and associated with an outrageous legend.

Where do monsters come from? Do they come from our collective psyche? Do they arise from genetic disorders? Are they the products of business expediency? Are they cobbled together from religious, ethnic, and political intolerance? The story of the Jersey Devil results from all of this, but it also derives from the story of a family thrown onto the pyre of popular culture mostly by people who had no idea of what they were doing.

Blank slates are the easiest to write on. By virtue of his publications being lost, intentionally destroyed, wiped away, and forgotten, the memory of Daniel Leeds and his family became an almost blank slate. Most of the "facts" attached to the Jersey Devil legend have nothing to do with reality. As with so many historical personages, much about the Leedses has been lost and covered over; even their final resting places are unknown. The disappearance of Daniel Leeds extends not only to his books and ephemeral works but also to his body. It is widely accepted that he was buried in the cemetery of St. Mary's in Burlington. A search of church archives and the grounds themselves, however, show no signs that he is interred there. Likewise, his father, Thomas Leeds, long thought buried in the Quaker burial grounds at Shrewsbury, New Jersey, has no records or headstone verifying that fact. Titan's grave also remains elusive.[1]

The Jersey Devil, on the other hand, still lives. Saying the story no longer has any relevance or interest, as Charles Montgomery Skinner did in 1903, underestimates the enduring character of the tale. Enthusiasts will continue to traipse around the forest looking for a monster, and eyewitnesses will continue to swear they have seen the creature cavorting among the pines. Myth often has a longer life span than reality, and so much reality surrounding this story has been forgotten. Priorities of the narrative, as they always do, have changed over the course of time.

The quarrels, fights, and animosities that seemed so important in the eighteenth century no longer held sway in the nineteenth. The Quaker rivalries, the political wrestling, the almanac wars, Daniel, Titan, and the monstrous Leeds family crest faded from memory, like paint chips flaking away from a wall mural, leaving a distorted version of the original image. The texts through which this conflict played out passed into obscurity, leaving little behind to tell the real story. Leeds's scandal-ridden writings—*The Trumpet Sounded* and *The Great Mystery of Fox-Craft*—attacked Quakerism and its founder and resulted in the destruction of many of the Leeds's publications. As prominent citizens, both Daniel and Titan must have engaged in extensive correspondence, yet virtually none of it survives. Through their public battles with publishing rivals, Daniel found himself accused of being Satan's harbinger, while Benjamin Franklin accused Titan Leeds of being a ghost resurrected from the grave. Daniel Leeds, by virtue of his supposed heresy, his breaking with the Quaker community to join the opposition, his outspoken anti-Quaker views, his almanac writing, and his siding with the royal government, made him a political and religious monster to his neighbors.

By the early twentieth century, the Leeds Devil and its fragile memory, remodeled by sensational media reportage, had become the Jersey Devil, while Mother Leeds, as much a phantom as her offspring, materialized out of the snow-covered forests surrounding Leeds Point. The Jersey Devil came into being from the collision of several different streams of history. The religious strife and bare-knuckled political maneuverings of the Keithian Schism and the pamphlet and almanac wars of the colonial era placed Daniel and Titan Leeds in a position to be accused of occult activity. This later melded nicely with the Native American traditions of forest dragons and spiritual beings to produce the Leeds Devil, which in turn found itself modified by a legion of other monster legends from home and abroad. By the turn of the twentieth century, this legend—now completely divorced from the actual Leeds family—was grafted onto strange tracks in the snow and then promoted by a dime museum.

When Charles Bradenburgh and Norman Jeffries constructed the Jersey Devil myth, they did not maliciously intend to tarnish the Leeds family name or an important part of American history. Nor did they think they had created a long-running legend. They just wanted to lure paying rubes to their funhouse. The story continued to be propagated by amateur folklorists, such as Francis Bazley Lee and particularly Henry Charlton Beck. Since then, a legion of ghost and monster hunters have pursued the case by looking for an actual biological entity they think has been alive since 1735. At the same time, the paranormal echo chamber combined with social media outlets to spread stories that paid little attention to verification, facts, veracity, or even common sense.

Today you need not go to the Pine Barrens to hear the call of the Jersey Devil. You can hear it while watching misleading political attack ads or reality television or internet hype about ghosts, monsters, or other pseudoscientific claims. The Jersey Devil whispers a warning, not about the horrors of darkened forests, but of darkened hearts. It warns against false accusations, the demonizing of political opponents or individuals because of their differences, of scapegoating, and about the tragedy of lost and forgotten history.

Ghost hunters and monster enthusiasts have traveled the back roads of the Pine Barrens for years and have reported encountering many unusual things. One of the great curiosities of the hunt for the Jersey Devil is that, with all the sightings of footprints and glowing red eyes, the hearing of shrill screams, and the photographing of strange beasts fluttering about the forests of New Jersey, no one has ever reported the ghost of a man in Quaker garb. If they want to be historically accurate, monster hunters might consider that the apparitions they think they see are not of some winged phantasm, but of the forlorn figure of Daniel Leeds standing on a lonely, tree-lined trail as the snow falls.

Notes

Introduction

1. Leeds, *News of a Trumpet Sounded Out*, pref.

Chapter 1. "Let this one be a Devil!"

1. For the folk life of New Jersey, see Cohen, *The Folklore and Folklife of New Jersey*.

2. McPhee, *The Pine Barrens*, 75.

3. This name is sometimes spelled *Nova Caesarea*.

4. Thomas, *History of Pennsylvania and West-Jersey*, 1. Thomas gives a detailed description of West Jersey, including information about crops, plants, the Native people, and the weather. He discusses flying squirrels and other creatures, even mentioning bears, though he points out that bears are not dangerous to humans. Like all the authors who wrote about New Jersey in this period, he nowhere mentions a Leeds Devil or any other type of forest monster.

5. Pestana, "The City upon a Hill under Siege, 323–353.

6. Lurie and Veit, *New Jersey*.

7. For more on the Native people of this region, see Grumet, *The Munsee Indians*, Thompson, *The Contest for the Delaware Valley*, and Soderlund, *Lenape Country*.

8. Wacker, *Land and People*.

9. DeLaet, "New World."

10. According to Herbert C. Kraft, *M'Sing* was correctly spelled *Mesingw* and alternately spelled with several variations, including *M'Sing*. Many alternate names exist in the anthropological literature, including "Living Solid Face," "Masked Keeper," and "Keeper of the Game." See Kraft, *The Lenape*.

11. Harrington, "Some Customs of the Delaware Indians," 55.

12. Beck, *Jersey Genesis*. See also McPhee, *The Pine Barrens*, 68.

13. Winick, "Tales of the Jersey Devil." Frank Esposito also cited the Vance Larner description in his 1978 book *Travelling New Jersey*, 89–90.

14. The name given to an evil spirit was *Mahtantu*, but this was not considered a devil by the Lenape. See Kraft, *The Lenape*, 163.

15. Lawrence Snake, video interview, by Frank J. Esposito, Anadarko, Oklahoma, March 18, 1993.

16. Lindstrom, *Geographia Americae*, 176.

17. Ibid.

18. Kraft, *The Lenape*, 178, quotes Lindstrom, *Geographia Americae*, 207–208, to support this.

19. Speck, *A Study of the Delaware Indian Big House Ceremony*, Weslager, *The Del-*

aware Indians, 75, and Esposito, "Indian-White Relations in New Jersey, 1609–1802," 28–29.

20. Kraft, *The Lenape Indian–Delaware Heritage,* 493. For a firsthand description of the Big House ceremony, see Dean, "Remembrance of the Big House Church," 41–49. See also Esposito, "The Anadarko Delaware of Oklahoma," 59–62, and Newcomb, *The Culture of Acculturation of the Delaware Indians,* 60.

21. Marsh, "Principal Characteristics of American Pterodactyls." Also see Harrington, "Some Customs of the Delaware Indians," 57.

22. Widmer, *The Geology and Geography of New Jersey,* 117–120.

23. Marsh, "Principal Characteristics of American Pterodactyls," 479–480.

24. *Newark News,* 1967.

25. Regensburg, *Evidence of Indian Settlement Patterns in the Pine Barrens,* and Cavallo and Mounier, "Aboriginal Settlement Patterns in the New Jersey Pine Barrens," 68–100.

26. *Laws of the General Assembly of East Jersey,* 1668. See also *The New Jersey Law Journal* 17, 1894, for witchcraft references.

27. Leaming and Spicer, *The Grants, Concessions, and Original Constitutions of the Province of New Jersey,* 80, 106.

28. *Pennsylvania Gazette,* October 15–22, 1730.

29. McCloy and Miller, *The Jersey Devil.*

30. Zeisberger, in Hulbert and Schwarze, *History of the North American Indians,* 127.

31. C. A. Weslager, *Magic Medicines of the Indians* (Middle Atlantic Press, 1973), 132, and Speck, "The Memorial Brush Heap in Delaware and Elsewhere," 17–23.

32. Speck, *A Study of Delaware Indian Medicine Practices,* 41.

33. Daston and Park, *Wonders and the Order of Nature.*

34. Crawford, *Marvelous Protestantism,* 30–35.

35. For the life of Anne Hutchinson and the Antinomian Controversy, see Battis, *Saints and Sectaries,* and Winship, *Making Heretics.*

36. Modern medicine calls this a *hydatidiform mole.*

37. Buchanan, "A Study of Maternal Rhetoric," 239–259.

38. Pearl and Pearl, "Governor John Winthrop on the Birth of the Antinomians' 'Monster,'" 21–37.

39. *The Register of the New Jersey Society of the Colonial Dames of America* (Trenton, NJ, 1914), 301.

40. Bonomi, *The Lord Cornbury Scandal.* The portrait still hangs in a place of honor at the New-York Historical Society, but the label says "portrait of an unknown woman."

Chapter 2. The Devil and Daniel Leeds

1. Smith, *The History of the Colony of Nova-Caeseria,* 151. Leeds and others were named to Cornbury's council because they were local men of importance within the community.

2. Regal, "The Jersey Devil, 50–53.

3. Confusion surrounds the details of Daniel's birth in England. He may have been born in Nottingham, or it may have been the town of Leeds in Kent (which is not the large industrial city of the North, also called Leeds). By the 1660s the family had moved to Stansted, north of London. Persecution of Quakers may have forced his parents to move around.

4. Leeds, *The Trumpet Sounded*, 143.

5. *Leeds Almanac* for 1712. This material, as well as some autobiographical material in *The Trumpet Sounded*, represents the few examples of his discussion of his early life in print. The run of various forms of the *Leeds Almanac* can be found as scanned facsimiles in the databases *Early American Imprints, Series 1: Evans, 1639–1880*, and EEBO (Early English Books Online).

6. *Boehme* is the commonest American spelling of this name. It can be found in the literature in several variations.

7. Leeds, *The Trumpet Sounded*, intro.

8. Essex County [UK] Records Office, Sessions Rolls, Easter 1666. Q/SR 408/93, March 18, 1666.

9. Leeds, *The Trumpet Sounded*, intro.

10. Essex County [UK] Records Office. Calendar of Essex Assize file [ASS 35/113/3] Assizes held at Chelmsford, July 15, 1672, ref. code T/A 418/175/25. Also see *Beach Haven Times* (Manahawkin, NJ), November 15, 1978, 6.

11. Leeds, *The Trumpet Sounded*, 4–6.

12. Researcher Joseph Hewlett argues, in "The Leeds Family of South Jersey," (Unpublished typescript in the collection of the Pennsylvania Historical Society, 1972), that the family emigrated from Nottinghamshire.

13. British National Archive, *Register of Burials belonging to the Quakers of the Burying Ground in Checker Alley in Whitecross Street in London*. RG6 Piece 499 Folio 0. Quaker founder George Fox is also buried here. Today the burial ground is a children's playground and garden maintained by the Friends, though there are a few signs that it was once a cemetery.

14. Several ships headed for New Jersey in 1677. These include the *Kent, Shield, Willing Minde*, and *Martha*. The incomplete extant records do not include the name *Leeds* in the passenger lists. The record for the *Shield* does list Thomas Revel, who was Daniel Leeds' best friend and later political ally, whose sister Jane became Daniel's last wife. This same passenger list also includes Mahlon Stacy, whose niece Ann was Daniel's first wife in America. Dates make the arrival narrative problematic. The *Kent* left England in May, but records show Daniel's mother Mary dying and being buried in London in July. Also, the *Shield* does not arrive in Burlington until December 1677. Records indicate that Thomas Sr. married Margaret Collier in August in Burlington. Indeed, Thomas's marriage to Margaret is officially known as the first Quaker wedding in Burlington. Finally, Daniel signed the *Concessions and Agreements*, which is dated March 1677. See Sheppard, *Passengers and Ships Prior to 1684*, and Smith, *His-*

tory of the Colony of Novo-Caesaria. In addition, Smith lists the year as 1677 in the body of his text, yet in the index it says 1676. The reality is that it is unknown how or when exactly the Leeds family came to America.

15. The *Dictionary of American Biography* throws up its hands and simply says the family arrived "sometime in the third quarter of the seventeenth century" (vol. 11, ed. Dumas Malone (New York: Charles Scribner's Sons, 1933), 135.

16. Griscom, *The Historic County of Burlington,* 1–2.

17. Morgan Hills, *History of the Church in Burlington,* 10. This structure, with its beautiful interior, still stands.

18. Biddle, *William and Sarah Biddle,* 92–94.

19. McMahon, *South Jersey Towns,* 210.

20. Gillespie, in Brunvand, *American Folklore,* 408.

21. Burlington Court Records; *Stillwell's Miscellany* 2: 18, 23, 41, 44, 45.

22. *Patents and Deeds and Other Early Records.*

23. *Atlantic County Historical Society Yearbook* 1:1 (1948): 8–14.

24. Lee, *Genealogical and Memorial History,* 1609–1611, and Humeston, *Leeds.*

25. Capp, *English Almanacs,* 275–276.

26. Harry Woolf, "Science for the People: Copernicanism and Newtonianism in the Almanacs of Early America," in J. Dobrzyki, *The Reception of Copernican Heliocentric Theory* (Baltimore: Johns Hopkins University Press, 1973).

27. Pomfret, *The Province of West New Jersey,* 233.

28. Dyer, *A Biography of James Parker.* Also see Felcone, *Printing in New Jersey.*

29. Quoted in Murray, *History of Education in New Jersey,* 15–16.

30. Isaiah Thomas, *A History of Printing in America* (Worchester, MA, 1810), 209. The fact that Bradford printed Daniel Leeds's almanac gives some weight to the notion that Bradford may have had his press in Burlington before moving it across the Delaware to Philadelphia.

31. Thomas Budd, *Good Order Established in Pennsylvania and New-Jersey* (n.p., [London?], 1685). As with so many authors of the era, although Budd discusses the flora and fauna of New Jersey, he makes no mention of a forest dragon.

32. *Reading Eagle,* February 1, 1926. Also see Livingston Rowe Schuyler, "Liberty of the Press," *Magazine of History with Notes and Queries* (New York) (June–December, 1905): 55–65.

33. On the history of English almanacs, see Curth, *English Almanacs.*

34. See various almanacs, such as Jeffrey Netie's *An Almanacke for the Year of Our Lord 1621,* in the John Johnson Collection, Bodleian Library, Oxford, England.

35. Daniel Leeds, *An Almanac, 1687* (Philadelphia, 1687).

36. Shinn, *The History of the Shinn Family,* 53.

37. *Leeds Almanac* for 1713.

38. Minutes from December 15, 1704, *Extracts from the Minutes of the Meeting of Friends,* Woodbridge, New Jersey, 1606–1751. New Jersey Historical Society, MG68, folder 1.

39. Quoted in Shinn, *The History of the Shinn Family.*

40. Hildebrun, "The First Book Printed South of Massachusetts," 461–462.

41. Thomas Budd's *Good Order Established*, which is dated 1685, may have been published in London rather than Philadelphia, but there is some controversy over its place of origin. See the introduction by Frederick J. Shepard in the 1902 Burrows Bros. edition.

42. Leeds, *The Temple of Wisdom*, 67.

43. Ibid., pref.

44. Ibid., 7, 1, 22.

45. Ibid., 65–67.

46. Stoudt, *Jacob Boehme*, Versluis, *Wisdom's Children*, and DeFoort. "Monstrosity in 17th-Century German Theosophy."

47. Gibbons, *Gender in Mystical and Occult Thought*.

48. Leeds, *Temple of Wisdom*, intro.

49. John Heydon, *Theomagia; or, the Temple of Wisdome in Three Parts, Spiritual, Celestial, and Elemental, Containing the Occult Powers of the Angels* (London, 1664). Printed by the same print shop "at the Gun" in London that printed Leeds's *Trumpet Sounded out of the Wilderness* in 1699.

50. Versluis, *The Esoteric Origins of the American Renaissance*, 21–24.

51. Murray, *History of Education in New Jersey*, 14.

52. Leeds, *Temple of Wisdom*, 118.

53. Monod, *Solomon's Secret Arts*.

54. Tomlin, "Astrology's from Heaven not Hell," 289.

55. Hutchenson, "What Happened to Occult Qualities in the Scientific Revolution?," 233–253.

56. Cadbury, "Early Quakerism and Uncanonical Lore," 177–205. Also see Frost, "Quaker Books in Colonial Pennsylvania," 1–23.

57. Gladfelter, "Power Challenged," 116–144.

58. "Commentary on Jacob Behmen and the Temple of Wisdom," Misc. Mss Boxes B, 1650, *American Antiquarian Society*. This letter, which has no name or date, may have come from the collection of Increase Mather. Its provenance is unclear, though it was written to Leeds during his lifetime.

59. This is in the collection of the Pennsylvania Historical Society.

60. *Athenian Mercury* (London), October 6, 1694, 3. Some of the few remaining examples of the work of Daniel Leeds survive in English collections. Oxford's Bodleian Library has a copy of *The Trumpet Sounded*, as does the British Library, in London. The British Library also has fragments of one of the few remaining copies of the original 1687 *Leeds Almanac*.

61. Miller and Pencal, *Pennsylvania*, Fisher, "Prophesies and Revelations," 299–333, and Seidensticker, "The Hermits of the Wissahickon," 427–441.

62. Gummere, *Witchcraft and Quakerism*, 52. Quaker scholar Amelia Mott Gummere felt that Leeds had some direct contact with Johannes Kelpius and the Wissahickon group, though evidence of this is thin.

63. *Leeds Almanac* for 1694.

64. Today the moon is known to be 238,900 miles from Earth.

65. All of these quotes from Daniel Leeds, *Almanac for 1693* (Philadelphia, 1692).

66. *Leeds Almanac*, 1695.

67. Johnson, "Thomas Digges, the Copernican System, and the Idea of the Infinity of the Universe in 1576," 69–117.

68. Wilding, "The Return of Thomas Salusbury's Life of Galileo," 241–265.

69. Ibid., 420.

70. Kassel, *Medicine and Magic in Elizabethan London.*

71. *Leeds Almanac* for 1695.

72. *Burlington County Supreme Court Records*, 1681–1709, 7. New Jersey State Archives.

73. Burr, *The Anglican Church in New Jersey*, 34–45. Also see O'Connor, *Three Centuries of Mission.*

74. Leeds, *The Trumpet Sounded*, 5.

75. Caleb Pusey, *A Modest Account from Philadelphia*, 38–39.

76. Leeds, *The Innocent Vindicated*, 3. This work was published in England in 1699 so that the London Friends could feel Leeds's wrath as well.

77. Keith later responded with *The Anti-Christ's and Sadducees Detailed Among a Sort of Quaker; or, Caleb Pusey of Pennsylvania and John Pennington* (1696).

78. Leeds, *The Trumpet Sounded.*

79. Ibid., 5.

80. Ibid., 141.

81. *Leeds Almanac* for 1697.

82. *Minutes of the Burlington Monthly Meeting*, July 1, 1698.

Chapter 3. The Devil and the Founding Father

1. This work is also known as *The Battle Door for Teachers and Professors* and is a peculiar defense of the Quaker use of the words *thee* and *thou.*

2. Leeds, *Trumpet Sounded*, 110.

3. Anonymous, *The Case Put and Decided* (New York, 1699). This work is often credited to Daniel Leeds.

4. Jennings, *Truth Rescued from Forgery and Falsehood.*

5. Rachel P. Leys, "Caleb Pusey and His Time," *Proceedings of the Delaware County Historical Society* (Chester, PA: 1902), 1:125–129. As William Bradford had followed George Keith and Daniel Leeds away from the Quakers, another Philadelphia printer, the Dutch-born Reynier Jansen (d.1706), picked up the slack and became a de facto Friends printer. Frost, "Unlikely Controversialists," 16–36, and Riewald, *Reynier Jansen of Philadelphia.*

6. Pennington, *Apostle of New Jersey.*

7. Morgan Hills, *History of the Church in Burlington*, 226, 716.

8. Quoted in Schermerhorn, *History of Burlington New Jersey*, 53.

9. *The Spirit of Missions* (New York, 1916), 81:286. Also see Pusey, *Some Remarks Upon a Late Pamphlet.*

10. McFarland, *Recovering John Talbot*. This excellent, though self-published, work exists in only a few copies.

11. Leeds, *The Great Mystery of Fox-Craft Discovered*. See also Versluis, *The Esoteric Origins of the American Renaissance*, 21.

12. Sheridan, *Lewis Morris, 1671–1746*.

13. Quoted in Morgan Hills, *History of the Church in Burlington*, 56.

14. Pusey, *False News from Gath Rejected*.

15. Leeds, *A Challenge to Caleb Pusey*, 1.

16. Pusey, *The Bomb Search'd and Found*, 75.

17. Pusey, *Satan's Harbinger Encountered*.

18. Leeds, *A Challenge to Caleb Pusey*, 1.

19. Leeds, *News of a Strumpet*, 1. This pamphlet is only known from one extant copy, which contains the signature of Daniel Leeds.

20. Bonomi, *The Lord Cornbury Scandal*, 122.

21. *The Register of the New Jersey Society of the Colonial Dames of America* (Trenton, NJ, 1914), 301.

22. On the Taylor-Walker feud, see Inglis, "Behaving Badly in the Press."

23. Olson, "Monster of Monsters," 1–22.

24. Thumb, *The Monster of Monsters*.

25. Ely, *The Deformity of a Hideous Monster*.

26. Quotes in Stowell, "American Almanacs and Feuds," 276–285.

27. Taylor, *Ephemeris Sideralis for 1705*.

28. Gadbury, *Ephemerides of the Celestial Motions*.

29. Geneva, *Astrology and the Seventeenth-Century Mind*. Also see Gadbury, *Collectio Genturarum*.

30. Gadbury, *De Cometis*.

31. Shields, "The Wits and Poets of Philadelphia," 99–143.

32. Jacob Taylor, *Almanac for the Year 1705*. Also see Phillips, "Certain Almanacs Published between 1705 and 1744," 291–297.

33. Arbour, "The First North American Mathematical Book," 87–98.

34. *A Collection of Memorials*, 69.

35. Smith, *The History of the Colony of Nova-Caeseria*, 284, 293.

36. In 1655 the Dutch astronomer Christian Huygens (1629–95) discovered a moon orbiting Saturn; he called it Titan. So inspired, Daniel Leeds paid homage by naming his son after it.

37. *Leeds Almanac* for 1714.

38. Collins, "The Friends at Leeds Point," 28–31.

39. Mather, *The Armour of Christianity*.

40. Quoted in Gummere, *Witchcraft and Quakerism*, 20.

41. Saunders, *Astrological Judgement and Practice of Physic*.

42. For a brief discussion of this, see Isaacson. *Benjamin Franklin*, 95–97.

43. Pencak, "Politics of Ideology in 'Poor Richard's Almanack,'" 183–211.

44. *Poor Richard's Almanac*, transcribed in Smith, *The Writings of Benjamin Franklin*, 2:196.

45. *Poor Richard's Almanac*, 1733.

46. October 18, 1733. Reprinted in Smith, *The History of the Colony of Nova-Caeseria*, 196.

47. *Poor Richard's Almanac*, 1735, in ibid.

48. Benjamin Franklin, *Pennsylvania Gazette*, February 4, 1738.

49. *Poor Richard's Almanac*, 1742.

50. Le May, *The Life of Benjamin Franklin*, 389. For an excellent analysis of Franklin's skill in writing, see Weinberger, *Benjamin Franklin Unmasked*, 100–134.

51. See Levine, "Early American Literature," 429–431, and Maestro, "Benjamin Franklin and the Penal Laws," 551–562.

52. *Felix Leeds Almanac* for 1727.

53. See Hewlett, "The Leeds Family of South Jersey." Unpublished typescript in the collection of the Pennsylvania Historical Society, 1972.

54. Thanks to the Royal College of Arms, London, and researcher Timothy Duke for his time and effort.

55. *American Weekly Herald* 752 (May 23, 1734).

56. Existing copies of the Leeds/American Almanac after about 1743 are fragmentary.

57. "Pension Papers of Jeremiah Leeds," *Atlantic County Historical Society Yearbook* 2:1 (1952): 198–203.

58. Ibid.,198.

59. 1784 Final Muster Roll, 3rd Battalion, Gloucester County Infantry, New Jersey State Archives.

60. Blake, "Family Records of Jeremiah Leeds," 203–206.

Chapter 4. The Birth of the Jersey Devil

1. *The Universal Calendar and North American Almanac* (Vermont, 1788).

2. Smith, *History of the Colony of Nova Caesarea*, chap. 3.

3. Semonin, *American Monster*.

4. Home, "Some Account of the Fossil Remains," 512–513.

5. Home, "Reasons for Giving the Name Proteo-Saurus, 113.

6. Henry de la Beche and William Conybeare, "Notice of the Discovery of a New Fossil Animal, Forming a Link between the Ichthyosaurus and the Crocodile ... ," *Transactions of the Geological Society of London* 5 (1821): 559–594.

7. Gatschet, "Water Snakes of American Aborigines," 255–260, quote on 256.

8. O'Neil, *The Great New England Sea-serpent*.

9. "The New England Sea-serpent," *Western Folklore* 7:1 (1948): 67.

10. Humphreys, *Letters from the Hon. David Humphreys*, 8.

11. Ibid., 23.

12. Ibid., 83.

13. Brown, "A Natural History of the Gloucester Sea Serpent," 402–436. Worse yet, in 1818 a local ship captain named Rich found the creature. The sightings had a familiar ring to him. He and his crew went out on calm days and discovered that the source of the sightings was a large, but common, mackerel.

14. Gosse, *The Romance of Natural History*, 311.

15. See Greene, *American Science in the Age of Jefferson*, Hindle, The *Pursuit of Science in Revolutionary America*, and Struit, *Yankee Science in the Making*.

16. See Regal, "Nuns on the Run," 34–39. There are some in the Christian Fundamentalist world who continue to believe that the Runaway Nun stories were genuine, despite the considerable evidence to the contrary.

17. Goodman, *The Sun and the Moon*. Also see Regal, "When Beavers Roamed the Moon," 28–30.

18. Following the success of the Moon Hoax, Locke tried again with *The Lost Manuscript of Mungo Park*. This story told the exciting tale of a Scottish explorer, but it did not do as well. The Moon Hoax did supposedly undermine Edgar Allan Poe, who had been writing his own moon story, *Hans Pfaall* (1835).

19. For the Cardiff Giant, see Tribble, *A Colossal Hoax*. For the other giants, see "Cheats and Hoaxes Recalled," *Salt Lake Tribune*, June 7, 1908, 17, and "Cardiff Giant Fraud," *Salt Lake Herald* 235, April 23, 1899, 9.

20. Bondeson, *The Feejee Mermaid and Other Essays*, 36–63.

21. Paijmans, "The Devil Kid of Newburg," 28–29.

22. Paijmans, "New Jersey's Spring Heeled Jack Scare," 28–29.

23. See *New York Tribune*, August 31, 1884, 9, *Phillipsburg Herald* (Kansas), October 2, 1884, *Wichita Eagle*, November 14, 1884, and *New North-West* (Montana), November 28, 1884.

24. McPhee, *The Pine Barrens*.

25. "Devil in New Jersey," *National Republican*, March 10, 1884, 4.

26. McPhee, *The Pine Barrens*, 73.

27. "The Engineer Quit His Run," *New York Sun*, January 22, 1893.

28. "Leeds Devil Returns," *St. Paul Globe* (St. Paul, MN), July 16, 1899.

29. "Jersey Sees a Devil," *Akron Daily Democrat*, August 5, 1899, 8.

30. Skinner, *American Myths and Legends*, 243.

31. "The Devil was Bordentown Born," *Trenton Times*, July 15, 1905, 2.

32. "Fly Rival of 'Leeds Devil' Has Jersey People Frightened," *Trenton Evening Times*, January 20, 1909, 1.

33. Ken Finkel, *Philly History Blog*, "The Skeleton, the Jersey Devil, and a Multitude of Other Attractions," accessed December 12, 2012.

34. *Sporting and Theatrical Journal*, March 22, 1884.

35. *Philadelphia Inquirer*, September 13, 1886.

36. Dennett, *Weird and Wonderful*. The building eventually came down. Today it is a parking lot.

37. "Fly Rival of 'Leeds Devil' Has Jersey People Frightened," 1.

38. "The Things They See in Jersey," *New York Tribune*, October 20, 1909.

39. "Real 'Jersey Devil' Found," *New Ulm Review* (New Ulm, MN), October 27, 1909, 7.

40. "The Trail of the Jersey Devil," *Philadelphia Evening Public Ledger*, January 19, 1918, 6, and T.A.D., "On the Trail of the Jersey Devil," *Philadelphia Public Ledger*, January 9, 1918.

41. Watson Buck, quoted in Reed, *Mother Leeds' Thirteenth Child*.

42. "South Jersey Joke Ended," *New York Times*, January 23, 1909, and "Scoff at Report of Jersey Devil," *Chester Times* (Chester, PA), January 23, 1932, 8.

43. "The Trail of the Jersey Devil."

44. "Hot Pursuit of the Jersey Bombat," *Columbian* (Bloomsbury, PA), June 24, 1909, 2.

45. *Columbian* (Bloomsbury, PA), June 24, 1909, 6. Some months later this story appeared in Chicago: "Battled with a Bird," *Chicago Eagle*, September 11, 1909.

46. "Jersey Devil Dead," *Daily Press* (Newport News, VA), October 31, 1909, 11.

Chapter 5. The Devil's Biographers

1. Cloy and Miller, *Phantom of the Pines*.

2. Though it is often cited, particularly by McCloy and Miller in *Phantom of the Pines* (1998), the diary is of spurious origins. A number of researchers have tried to track down the Larner manuscript without success. Our contacts with numerous manuscript depositories, including the Library of Congress, where the entire database was searched, have uncovered no record of its existence. The New Jersey manuscript depositories of both Rutgers and Rowan Universities, as well as the New Jersey Historical Society and the Newark Public Library, have no record of the diary's existence. Until further evidence comes along it must be treated as a hoax. See Nigroni, "The Vance Larner Diary," 10–12, and Winick, "Tales of the Jersey Devil."

3. Winick, "Tales of the Jersey Devil."

4. Smith, *The History of the Colony of Nova-Caeseria*, and Kalm, *Travels into North America*.

5. Mayer, "In the Pines," 560–569.

6. Ibid., 566.

7. Mayer also makes the first reference to Steven Decatur and his setting up of an iron foundry in the Pine Barrens to forge the cannons he would use in the war of the Barbary Pirates of North Africa. Mayer says that Decatur and his men made repeated test firings of their guns into the woods and that this scared many woodland creatures. He does not, however, make any connection between Decatur and the Leeds Devil. A later popular story relates how Decatur fired a cannon at the Jersey Devil. This story persists in the mythos even though there are no known accounts of this ever having happened. It seems likely that the written genesis of modern Leeds/Jersey Devil knowledge comes from Mayer, who simply passed along an odd story told by odd people from the woods of New Jersey, a tale that harked back to colonial times.

8. *New York Sun*, October 2, 1887, 5.

9. "The Engineer Quit His Run," *New York Sun*, January 22, 1893.

10. Obituary of Francis Bazley Lee, *New York Times*, May 3, 1914.

11. Lee, *Genealogical and Memorial History*, 1609–1612.

12. Watkins, "Demon of the Pines."

13. Marcus, "Obituary of J. Elfreth Watkins," 300–301.

14. Oddly, Watkins's article appeared in the September 1905 edition of the *Evening Star*, two years after his death. This may have been because the paper had the article and found space to print it only later, when the snowy footprint reports began to come in. It was in 1905 that the commotion about devils in the woods began in earnest.

15. Arminius Alba, "The Devil Was Bordentown Born," *Trenton Times*, July 15, 1905, 2.

16. Beck, *More Forgotten Towns of Southern New Jersey*, 116–117.

17. T.A.D., "On the Trail of the Jersey Devil," *Philadelphia Public Ledger*, January 9, 1918, 6.

18. *WPA Guide to 1930s New Jersey*.

19. McCloy and Miller, *The Jersey Devil*.

20. McMahon, *South Jersey Towns*, 212; also see Gillespie, "The (Jersey) Devil Is in the Details," 40–43. These are blind references to the spurious Vance Larner Diary.

21. Coleman and Hallenbeck, *The Monsters of New Jersey*, and McMahon, *South Jersey Towns*. To date, the best book on the Jersey Devil is Bill Sprouse's *The Domestic Life of the Jersey Devil* (2013). He includes a discussion of Daniel Leeds's publishing work and the religious and political aspects of the time. Sprouse places all this within the context of his own life and his relationship to his grandmother, who told him, when he was a child, that he is related to the Jersey Devil, inspiring him to go on a quest. As Beck did before him, Sprouse made his memoir a personal memoir rather than a scholarly treatise, albeit a more entertaining one. His book is the exception, however, to the field of Jersey Devil studies.

22. Heartman, *Preliminary Checklist of Almanacs*.

23. Felcone, *Printing in New Jersey*.

24. "Old Almanacs," *Trenton State Gazette*, December 13, 1848, 3.

25. Hall, *Daily Union History of Atlantic County*, 407–415.

26. Humeston, *Leeds: A New Jersey Family*, 3. See also Heston, "The Leeds Family," 9–11.

27. *Boston Evening Transcript*, December 4, 1912, 23. Authorship of this particular tract is unclear. There is no author printed, but Daniel Leeds signed the copy, so it is attributed to him.

28. Russet, "Legend of the Jersey Devil," 3. *Webster's II New Riverside Dictionary* (Boston: Riverside Publishing, 1994), 648.

29. Watson Buck, in Reed, *Mother Leeds' Thirteenth Child*.

30. "Posse Sets Out as 'Jersey Devil' Reappears; Black and Shaggy This Time, It Kills Hogs," *New York Times*, December 19, 1929.

31. "'Jersey Devil' Returns as Applejack Mellows, and Dry Agents Investigate the Coincidence," *New York Times*, August 6, 1930.

32. MacFadden, "Claws, Hoof, and Foot," 5–14.

33. Ibid. 31.

34. McCloy and Miller correctly identify the Decatur story as a "legend," *Phantom of the Pines*, 13.

35. The sightings of 1909 certainly meet the criteria of what represents mass hysteria. See McCloy and Miller, *Phantom of the Pines*, 29–41, for a detailed reporting of the chaos in 1909.

36. Russet, "Legend of the Jersey Devil," 4. See also Erik Larsen, "105 Years Ago Something Terrorized South Jersey," *Asbury Park Press*, January 24, 2014, A8.

37. "Catch 'Jersey Devil,'" *San Juan Islander* (Friday Harbor, WA), July 14, 1911.

38. "Huge Freak Fish Puts Up a Fight," *Bourbon News* (Paris, KY), August 16, 1912.

39. *Evening World* (New York), October 10, 1921. This report appeared in the sports section, with other fishing-related stories.

40. "Strange Animal Is Chicken Thief," *Trenton Evening Times*, August 8, 1919.

41. "Bags 'What-is-it,'" *Philadelphia Evening Public Ledger*, April 10, 1920.

42. "Half-Witted Youth Says He Is Vandal-Burglar," *Philadelphia Evening Public Ledger*, November 20, 1914.

43. *Philadelphia Evening Public Ledger*, October 10, 1921.

44. McCloy and Miller, *Phantom of the Pines*, 93.

45. Reed, *Mother Leeds' Thirteenth Child*.

46. McCloy and Miller, *Phantom of the Pines*, 98.

47. See Stephen Winick, "Tales of the Jersey Devil."

48. Quoted in Ben Russet, "The Legend of the Jersey Devil."

49. Reed, *Mother Leeds' Thirteenth Child*.

50. Regal, "Richard Owen and the Sea Serpent," 65–68.

51. For Krantz's life, see Regal, *Searching for Sasquatch*.

52. MacFadden. "Claws, Hoof, and Foot," 5–14.

53. A cryptid is a creature that is not described by mainstream science but that has a mythical history, with at least some, albeit controversial, physical or circumstantial evidence for its existence. Bigfoot and the Loch Ness Monster are prime examples.

54. Arthur V. Keller, quoted in Fred Cicetti, "Here and There," *Camden Courier Post*, October 30, 1975.

Chapter 6. The Devil Becomes a Star

1. Thanks to Skeptical writer and researcher Blake Smith for use of the term *echo chamber*.

2. Parsons, "Some Account of a Sheep, 183–186.

3. Fissell, "Hairy Women and Naked Truths," 43–74.

4. *Bickerstaff's Boston Almanac for the Year 1785* (1784).

5. Luther and Melanchthon, *The Papal Ass of Rome*.

6. Ibid., 357.

7. Hoeniger and Hoeniger, *The Development of Natural History in Tudor England*.

8. Jacob Rueff, *De Conceptu et Generatione Hominis* (Zurich, 1554).

9. Bates, *Emblematic Monsters*, 75.

10. Dickie, "Ambroise Paré," 1143–1146.

11. See Paget, *Ambroise Paré and His Times*.

12. Packard, *The Life and Times of Ambroise Paré*.

13. Bates, *Emblematic Monsters*, 75.

14. Ibid.

15. Paré, *Des Monstres et Prodiges*, 3.

16. Park and Daston, "Unnatural Conceptions," 20–54.

17. Paré, *Des Monstres et Prodiges*, 12.

18. Barsi, *L'énigme de la chronique de Pierre Belon*, and Hoeniger and Hoeniger, *The Development of Natural History*, 49.

19. Liceti, *De Monstrorum Natura Causis et Differentiis*.

20. Lazzarini, "Wonderful Creatures," 415–431.

21. Leroi, *Mutants*, 71.

22. Francis Bacon, *The New Organon: or, True Directions concerning the Interpretation of Nature* (1620), chap. 29.

23. Patrick Boyton, *Snallygaster: The Lost Legend of Frederick County* (Privately printed, 2008).

24. See David J. Parkin, "In the Nature of the Human Landscape: Provenances in the Making of Zanzibari Politics," in J. Clammer, S. Poirier, and E. Schwimmer, eds., *Figured Worlds: Ontological Obstacles in Intercultural Relations* (Toronto: University of Toronto Press, 2004, 113–131, and "Terror, Tourism and Odd Beliefs," *Economist*, December 13, 2003, 57, and Radford, "Popobawa."

25. "The Face Painter," an episode in *Seinfeld*, May 11, 1995.

26. Springsteen himself was occasionally referred to as "The Jersey Devil" by some fans, but the moniker never really stuck.

Epilogue

1. This is not particularly unusual, as the Quakers did not always employ headstones.

Selected Bibliography

A Collection of Memorials Concerning Divers Deceased Ministers and Others of the People Called Quakers (Philadelphia, 1787).

Arbour, Keith. "The First North American Mathematical Book and Its Metalcut Illustrations: Jacob Taylor's Tenebrae, 1697." *Pennsylvania Magazine of History and Biography* 123:1–2 (1999).

Barsi, Monica, *L'énigme de la chronique de Pierre Belon*. Milan: Edizioni universitarie di lettere economia diritto, 2001.

Bates, A. W. *Emblematic Monsters: Unnatural Conceptions and Deformed Births in Early Modern Europe*. Amsterdam: Rodopi, 2005.

Battis, Emery. *Saints and Sectaries: Anne Hutchinson and the Antinomian Controversy in the Massachusetts Bay Colony*. Chapel Hill: University of North Carolina Press, 1962.

Beck, Henry Charlton. *Jersey Genesis: The Story of the Mullica River*. New Brunswick, NJ: Rutgers University Press, 1945.

Beck, Henry Charlton. *More Forgotten Towns of Southern New Jersey*. New Brunswick, NJ: Rutgers University Press, 1937.

Biddle, C. Miller. *William and Sarah Biddle, 1633–1711: Planting a Seed of Democracy in America*. Moorestown, NJ: By the author, 2012.

Blake, Georgiana C. "Family Records of Jeremiah Leeds." *Atlantic County Historical Society Yearbook* 2:1 (1952).

Bondeson, Jan. *The Feejee Mermaid and Other Essays on Natural and Unnatural History*. Ithaca, NY: Cornell University Press, 1999.

Bonomi, Patricia. *The Lord Cornbury Scandal: The Politics of Reputation in British America*. Chapel Hill: University of North Carolina Press, 2000.

Brown, C. M. "A Natural History of the Gloucester Sea Serpent." *American Quarterly* 42:3 (1990).

Buchanan, Lindal. "A Study of Maternal Rhetoric: Anne Hutchinson, Monsters, and the Antinomian Controversy." *Rhetoric Review* 25:3 (2006): 239–259.

Burr, Nelson R. *The Anglican Church in New Jersey*. Philadelphia: Church Historical Society, 1954.

Butler, Jon. "The Keithian Schism." *William and Mary Quarterly*, 3rd ser., 31:3 (1974): 431–452.

Cadbury, Henry J. "Early Quakerism and Uncanonical Lore." *Harvard Theological Review* 40:3 (1947).

Capp, Bernard. *English Almanacs: 1500–1800, Astrology and the Popular Press*. Ithaca, NY: Cornell University Press, 1979.

Cavallo, John A., and R. Alan Mounier. "Aboriginal Settlement Patterns in the New Jersey Pine Barrens." In *History, Culture, and Archaeology in the Pine Barrens: Essays from the Third Pine Barrens Conference*, edited by John W. Stinton, 68–100. Galloway, NJ: Center for Environmental Research, Stockton State College, 1980.

Cohen, David Steven. *The Folklore and Folklife of New Jersey*. New Brunswick, NJ: Rutgers University Press, 1983.

Coleman, Loren, and Bruce Hallenbeck. *The Monsters of New Jersey*. Mechanicsburg, PA: Stackpole Books. 2010.

Collins, Anna C. "The Friends at Leeds Point." Atlantic County Historical Society *Yearbook* 1:1 (1948).

Crawford, Julie. *Marvelous Protestantism: Monstrous Births in Post-Reformation England*. Baltimore: Johns Hopkins University Press, 2005.

Curth, Louise Hill. *English Almanacs: Astrology and Popular Medicine*. Manchester: Manchester University Press, 2007.

Daston, Lorraine J., and Katharine Park. *Wonders and the Order of Nature, 1150–1750*. Zone Books, 2001.

Dean, Nora Thompson. "Remembrance of the Big House Church." In *The Lenape Indian: A Symposium*. South Orange, NJ: Archaeological Research Center, Seton Hall University, 1984.

DeFoort, Filps. "Monstrosity in 17th-Century German Theosophy: The Case of Jacob Boehme (1575–1624)." *Monsters and the Monstrous* 1:1 (2011).

DeLaet, Johan. "New World." In *Narratives of New Netherland*, edited by J. Franklin Jameson. New York: Scribner's Sons, 1909.

Dennett, Andrea Stulman. *Weird and Wonderful: The Dime Museum in America*. New York: New York University Press, 1997.

Dickie, Francis. "Ambroise Paré: A Barber's Apprentice Who Became the Greatest Surgeon in History." *American Journal of Nursing* 31:10 (1931).

Dyer, Alan. *A Biography of James Parker, Colonial Printer, 1715–1770*. Albany, NY: Whitston Publishing, 1982.

Early American Imprints, Series 1: Evans, 1639–1880.

Ely, Samuel. *The Deformity of a Hideous Monster Discovered in the Province of Maine*. Boston, 1797.

Esposito, Frank J. "The Anadarko Delaware of Oklahoma." In *The Lenape Indian: A Symposium*. South Orange, NJ: Archaeological Research Center, Seton Hall University, 1984.

Esposito, Frank J. "Indian-White Relations in New Jersey, 1609–1802." PhD diss., Rutgers University, 1976.

Esposito, Frank J. *Travelling New Jersey*. Union, NJ: William H. Wise, 1978.

Felcone, Joseph J. *Printing in New Jersey: 1754–1800*. Worcester, MA: American Antiquarian Society, 2012.

Fisher, Elizabeth. "Prophesies and Revelations: German Cabbalists in Early Pennsylvania." *Pennsylvania Magazine of History and Biography* 109:3 (1985).

Fisher, Sydney George. *The True Benjamin Franklin*. Philadelphia: J. B. Lippincott, 1898.

Fissell, Mary E. "Hairy Women and Naked Truths: Gender and the Politics of Knowledge in Aristotle's Masterpiece," *William and Mary Quarterly* 60:1 (2007): 43–74.

Frost, J. William. "Quaker Books in Colonial Pennsylvania." *Quaker History* 80:1 (1991): 1–23.

Frost, J. William. "Unlikely Controversialists: Caleb Pusey and George Keith." *Quaker History* 64:1 (1975): 16–36.

Gadbury, John. *Collectio Genturarum.* London, 1662.

Gadbury, John. *De Cometis: A discourse on the nature and effects of comets.* London, 1665.

Gadbury, John. *Ephemerides of the Celestial Motions and Aspects of the Luninaries for 1682–1701.* London, 1680.

Gatschet, Albert S. "Water Snakes of American Aborigines." *Journal of American Folklore* 12:47 (1899): 255–260.

Geneva, Ann. *Astrology and the Seventeenth Century Mind: William Lilly and the Language of the Stars.* Manchester: Manchester University Press, 1995.

Gerhardus Riewald, Jacobus. *Reynier Jansen of Philadelphia, Early American Printer: A Chapter in 17th-Century Non-Conformity.* Groningen: Wolters-Noordhoff, 1970.

Gibbons, B. J. *Gender in Mystical and Occult Thought in Behmenism and Its Development in England.* Cambridge: Cambridge University Press, 1996.

Gillespie, Angus Kress. "Jersey Devil." In *American Folklore: An Encyclopedia,* edited by Jan Harold Brunvand, 408. New York: Routledge, 1998.

Gillespie, Angus Kress. "The (Jersey) Devil Is in the Details." *New Jersey Outdoors* (Fall 1933).

Gladfelter, Valerie G. "Power Challenged: Rising Individualism in the Burlington, New Jersey, Friends Meeting, 1678–1720." In *Friends and Neighbors: Group Life in America's First Plural Society,* edited by Michael Zuckerman. Philadelphia: Temple University Press, 1982.

Goodman, Matthew. *The Sun and the Moon: The Remarkable True Account of Hoaxers, Showmen, Dueling Journalists, and Lunar Man-Bats in Nineteenth-Century New York.* New York: Basic Books, 2008.

Gosse, Philip Henry. *The Romance of Natural History.* London: Gould & Lincoln, 1861.

Greene, John C. *American Science in the Age of Jefferson.* Ames: Iowa State University Press, 1984.

Griscom, Lloyd E. *The Historic County of Burlington.* Burlington: Burlington County Cultural and Heritage Commission, 1973.

Grumet, Robert. *The Munsee Indians: A History.* Norman: University of Oklahoma Press, 2009.

Gummere, Amelia Mott. *Witchcraft and Quakerism: A Study in Social History.* Philadelphia: Biddle Press, 1908.

Hall, John H. *Daily Union History of Atlantic County.* Atlantic City, NJ: Daily Union Printing, 1900.

Harrington, M. R. "Some Customs of the Delaware Indians." *Museum Journal* 1:3 (1910).

Heartman, Charles F. *Preliminary Checklist of Almanacs Printed in New Jersey Prior to 1850.* Metuchen, NJ, 1929.

Heston, Alfred H. "The Leeds Family." *Proceedings of the New Jersey Historical Society* 53 (1935).

Hildebrun, Charles R. "The First Book Printed South of Massachusetts." *Pennsylvania Magazine of History and Biography* 6:4 (1882).

Hindle, Brooke. *The Pursuit of Science in Revolutionary America, 1735–1789.* Chapel Hill: University of North Carolina Press, 1956.

Hoeniger, F. D., and J. F. M. Hoeniger. *The Development of Natural History in Tudor England.* Folger Books, 1979.

Home, Everard. "Reasons for Giving the Name Proteo-Saurus to the Fossil Skeleton Which Has Been Described," *Philosophical Transactions of the Royal Society* 2 (1815–1830).

Home, Everard. "Some Account of the Fossil Remains of an Animal More Nearly Aligned to Fishes than Any Other Classes of Animals," *Philosophical Transactions of the Royal Society* 1 (June 1814).

Humeston, Clara Louise. *Leeds: A New Jersey Family: Its Beginning and a Branchlet.* Voice Print, 1900[?].

Humphreys, David. *Letters from the Hon. David Humphreys to the Rt. Hon. Sir Joseph Banks Containing Some Account of the Serpent of the Ocean Frequently Seen in Gloucester Bay.* New York, 1817.

Hutchenson, Keith. "What Happened to Occult Qualities in the Scientific Revolution?" *Isis* 73:2 (1982).

Inglis, Kirsten. "Behaving Badly in the Press: John Taylor and Henry Walker, 1641–1643." *Transverse* 10 (2010).

Isaacson, Walter. *Benjamin Franklin: An American Life.* New York: Simon & Schuster, 2003.

Jennings, Samuell. *Truth Rescued from Forgery and Falsehood.* Philadelphia, 1699.

Johnson, Francis J. "Thomas Digges, the Copernican System, and the Idea of the Infinity of the Universe in 1576." *Huntington Library Bulletin* 5 (April 1934).

Kalm, Peter. *Travels into North America Containing Its Natural History.* Translated by John Reinhold Forster. London, 1771.

Kassel, Lauren. *Medicine and Magic in Elizabethan London.* Oxford: Clarendon Press, 2005.

Kirby, E. W. *George Keith.* New York: American Historical Association, 1942.

Kraft, Herbert C. *The Lenape: Archaeology, History, and Ethnography.* Newark: New Jersey Historical Society, 1986.

Kraft, Herbert C. *The Lenape Indian–Delaware Heritage: 10,000 BC to AD 2000.* Lenape Books. 2001.

Lang, Carole Ann. "Daniel Leeds: A Helpful Trouble-Maker." *South Jersey Magazine* (Summer 1999): 30.

Lazzarini, Elena. "Wonderful Creatures: Early Modern Perceptions of Deformed Bodies." *Oxford Art Journal* 34:3 (2011).

Leaming, Aaron, and Jacob Spicer. *The Grants, Concessions, and Original Constitutions of the Province of New Jersey.* Somerville, NJ, 1890.

Lee, Francis Bazley. *Genealogical and Memorial History of the State of New Jersey.* Vol. 4. New York: Lewis Historical Publishing, 1910.

Leeds, Daniel. *A Challenge to Caleb Pusey and a Check to His Lyes and Forgeries.* Philadelphia, 1700.

Leeds, Daniel. *News of a Strumpet Co-Habitating in the Wilderness.* Philadelphia, 1701.

Leeds, Daniel. *News of a Trumpet Sounded Out of the Wilderness of America.* New York, sold in London, 1699.

Leeds, Daniel. *The Great Mystery of Fox-Craft Discovered.* New York, 1705.

Leeds, Daniel, *The Innocent Vindicated from the Falsehoods and Slanders of Certain Certificates.* Philadelphia, 1695.

Leeds, Daniel. *The Rebuker Rebuked.* New York, 1703.

Leeds, Daniel. *The Second Part of the Mystery of Fox-Craft.* New York, 1705.

Leeds, Daniel. *The Temple of Wisdom for the Little World.* Philadelphia, 1688.

Leeds, Daniel. *The Trumpet Sounded out of the Wilderness of America.* Philadelphia, 1697.

Le May, J. A. Leo. *The Life of Benjamin Franklin, Printer and Publisher, 1730–1747.* Philadelphia: University of Pennsylvania Press, 2006.

Leroi, Armand Marie. *Mutants.* New York: Viking Press, 2003.

Levine, Robert S. "Early American Literature: A Comparatist Approach by A. Owen Aldridge." *Modern Philology* 82:4 (1985).

Liceti, Fortunio. *De Monstrorum Natura Causis et Differentiis.* 1616.

Lindstrom, Peter. *Geographia Americae: With An Account of the Delaware Indians Based on Surveys and Notes Made in 1654–1656.* Philadelphia: Swedish Historical Society, 1924.

Lurie, Maxine, and Richard Veit, eds. *New Jersey: A History of the Garden State.* New Brunswick, NJ: Rutgers University Press, 2012.

Luther, Martin, and Phillip Melanchthon. *The Papal Ass of Rome and the Monk Calf of Freyberg.* London, 1579.

MacFadden, Fred R. "Claws, Hoof, and Foot: The Devil's Tracks in Devon and New Jersey." *Free State Folklore* (Spring 1976).

Maestro, Marcello. "Benjamin Franklin and the Penal Laws." *Journal of the History of Ideas* 36:3 (1975).

Marcus, Benjamin. "Obituary of J. Elfreth Watkins." *Science* 18:453 (1903).

Marsh, O. C. "Principal Characteristics of American Pterodactyls." *American Journal of Science* (June 1876).

Mather, Cotton. *The Armour of Christianity: A treatise, detecting first, the plots of the devil against our happiness.* Boston, 1704.

Mayer, W. F. "In the Pines." *Atlantic Monthly* 3:19 (1859).

McCloy, James F., and Ray Miller Jr. *Phantom of the Pines: More Tales of the Jersey Devil.* Moorestown, NJ: Middle Atlantic Press, 1998.

McCloy, James F., and James Miller. *The Jersey Devil.* Wallingford, PA: Middle Atlantic Press, 1976.

McFarland, Cynthia. *Recovering John Talbot.* Burlington, NJ: Privately printed, 2011.

McMahon, William. *South Jersey Towns: History and Legend*. New Brunswick, NJ: Rutgers University Press, 1973.

McPhee, John. *The Pine Barrens*. New York: Farrar Straus & Giroux, 1981.

Miller, Randall, and William Pencal, eds. *Pennsylvania: A History of the Commonwealth*. University Park: Pennsylvania State University Press, 2002.

Monod, Paul Kleber. *Solomon's Secret Arts: The Occult in the Age of Enlightenment*. New Haven, CT: Yale University Press, 2013.

Morgan Hills, George. *History of the Church in Burlington, New Jersey*. Trenton, NJ: William Sharp, 1876.

Murray, David. *History of Education in New Jersey*. Washington, DC: Government Printing Office, 1899.

Netie, Jeffrey. *An Almanacke for the Year of Our Lord 1621*. London, 1620.

Newcomb, William J, Jr. *The Culture of Acculturation of the Delaware Indians*. Ann Arbor: University of Michigan, 1970.

Nigroni, Don. "The Vance Larner Diary." *Phactum* (July–August 2010).

O'Connor, Daniel. *Three Centuries of Mission*. London: Bloomsbury Academic, 2000.

O'Neill, J. P. *The Great New England Sea-serpent*. Camden, ME: Down East Books, 1999.

Olson, Alison, "'Monster of Monsters' and the Emergence of Political Satire in New England," *Historical Journal of Massachusetts* 29:1 (Winter 2001).

Packard, Francis R. *The Life and Times of Ambroise Paré*. New York: Paul B. Hoeber, 1921.

Paget, Stephen. *Ambroise Paré and His Times, 1510–1590*. New York: G. P. Putnam's Sons, 1897.

Paijmans, Theo. "New Jersey's Spring Heeled Jack Scare." *Fortean Times* 310 (February 2014).

Paijmans, Theo. "The Devil Kid of Newburg." *Fortean Times* 311 (March 2014).

Paré, Ambroise. *Des Monstres et Prodiges*. Translated by Janis L. Pallister. Chicago: University of Chicago Press, 1982.

Park, Katherine, and Lorraine Daston. "Unnatural Conceptions: The Study of Monsters in Sixteenth- and Seventeenth-Century France and England," *Past & Present* 92 (August 1981).

Parsons, James. "Some Account of a Sheep, Shewed Alive to the Royal Society, in November 1754, Having a Monstrous Horn Growing from His Throat; The Stuffed Skin of Which, with the Horn in Situ, Is Now in the Museum of the Society," *Philosophical Transactions* 49 (1755–56): 183–186.

Patents and Deeds and Other Early Records of New Jersey 1664–1703. Baltimore: Genealogical Publishing, 1976.

Pearl, Valerie, and Morris Pearl. "Governor John Winthrop on the Birth of the Antinomians' 'Monster': The Earliest Reports to Reach England and the Making of a Myth." *Proceedings of the Massachusetts Historical Society*, 3rd ser. 102 (1990): 21–37.

Pencak, William "Politics of Ideology in 'Poor Richard's Almanack.'" *Pennsylvania Magazine of History and Biography* 116:2 (1992).

Pennington, Edgar Legare. *Apostle of New Jersey, John Talbot, 1645–1727*. Philadelphia: Church Historical Society, 1938.

Pestana, Carla Gardine. "The City upon a Hill under Siege: The Puritan Perception of the Quaker Threat to Massachusetts Bay, 1656–1661." *New England Quarterly* 56:3 (1983): 323–353.

Phillips, Henry, Jr. "Certain Almanacs Published between 1705 and 1744." *Proceedings of the American Philosophical Society* 19:108 (1881).

Pomfret, John E. *The Province of West New Jersey*. New York: Octagon Books, 1976.

Pusey, Caleb. *A Modest Account from Philadelphia*. London: T. Sowle, 1696.

Pusey, Caleb. *False News from Gath Rejected*. Philadelphia, 1704.

Pusey, Caleb. *Satan's harbinger encountered, his false news of a trumpet detected, his crooked ways in the wildrnesse [sic] laid open to the view of the imperial and iudicious. Being something by way of answer to Daniel Leeds his book entituled News of a trumpet sounding in the wildernesse*. Philadelphia, 1700.

Pusey, Caleb. *Some Remarks Upon a Late Pamphlet Signed part by John Talbot, and part by Daniel Leeds, Called the Great Mystery of Fox-Craft*. Philadelphia, 1705.

Pusey, Caleb. *The Bomb Search'd and Found Stuffed with False Ingredients* (Philadelphia, 1705).

Radford, Benjamin. "Popobawa." *Fortean Times* 241 (October 2008).

Reed, Bill (producer). *Mother Leeds' Thirteenth Child*. New Jersey Public Broadcasting Company. Film. 1970.

Regal, Brian. "Nuns on the Run." *Fortean Times* 87 (June 1996).

Regal, Brian. "Richard Owen and the Sea Serpent." *Endeavour* 36:2 (2012).

Regal, Brian. *Searching for Sasquatch: Crackpots, Eggheads, and Cryptozoology*. New York: Palgrave Macmillan, 2013.

Regal, Brian. "The Jersey Devil: The Real Story." *Skeptical Inquirer* 57:6 (2013): 50–53.

Regal, Brian. "When Beavers Roamed the Moon." *Fortean Times* 109 (April 1998).

Regensburg, Richard. "Evidence of Indian Settlement Patterns in the Pine Barrens." Pomona, NJ: Stockton State College, 1978.

Riewald, Jacobus Gerhardus. *Reynier Jansen of Philadelphia, Early American Printer: A Chapter in 17th-Century Non-Conformity*. Groningen: Wolters-Noordhoff, 1970.

Russet, Ben. "The Legend of the Jersey Devil." In *The New Jersey Pine Barrens*. New York: Farrar, Straus & Giroux, 1978.

Saunders, Richard. *The Astrological Judgement and Practice of Physic*. 1677; repr., Astrology Classics, 2005.

Schermerhorn, William E. *History of Burlington New Jersey*. Burlington, NJ: Enterprise Publishing, 1927.

Seidensticker, Oswald. "The Hermits of the Wissahickon." *Pennsylvania Magazine of History and Biography* 11:4 (1888).

Semonin, Paul. *American Monster: How the Nation's First Prehistoric Creature Became a Symbol of National Identity.* New York: New York University Press, 2000.

Sheppard, Walter Lee, Jr. *Passengers and Ships Prior to 1684, Penn's Colony: Volume I* (1970) Westminster, MD: Heritage Books, 2007.

Sheridan, Eugene. *Lewis Morris, 1671–1746: A Study in Early American Politics.* Syracuse, NY: Syracuse University Press, 1981.

Shields, David S. "The Wits and Poets of Philadelphia: New Light on the Rise of Belle Lettres in Provincial Pennsylvania." *Pennsylvania Magazine of History and Biography* 109:2 (1985).

Shinn, Josiah H. *The History of the Shinn Family in Europe and America.* Chicago: Genealogical and Historical Publishing, 1903.

Skinner, Charles Montgomery. *American Myths and Legends.* Vol. 1. Philadelphia: J. B. Lippincott, 1903.

Smith, Albert Henry. *The Writings of Benjamin Franklin.* Vol. 2. New York: Macmillan, 1905.

Smith, Samuel. *The History of the Colony of Nova-Caeseria, or New Jersey.* Trenton, NJ: William S. Sharp, 1877.

Soderlund, Jean. *Lenape Country.* Philadelphia: University of Pennsylvania Press, 2014.

Speck, Frank G. *A Study of Delaware Indian Medicine Practices and Folk Beliefs.* Harrisburg: Pennsylvania Historical Commission, 1942.

Speck, Frank G. *A Study of the Delaware Indian Big House Ceremony.* Harrisburg, PA: Pennsylvania Historical Commission, 1931.

Speck, Frank G. "The Memorial Brush Heap in Delaware and Elsewhere." *Bulletin of the Archaeological Society of Delaware* 4 (1945): 17–23.

Sprouse, Bill. *The Domestic Life of the Jersey Devil; or, BeBop's Miscellany.* Margate City, NJ: Oyster Eye Publishing, 2013.

Stoudt, John Yost. *Jacob Boehme: His Life and Thought.* Eugene, OR: Wipf & Stock, 2004.

Stowell, Marion Barber. "American Almanacs and Feuds." *Early American Literature* 9:3 (1975).

Struit, Dirk Jan. *Yankee Science in the Making: Science and Engineering in New England from Colonial Times to the Civil War.* New York: Dover Publications, 1991.

Taylor, Jacob. *Ephemeris Sideralis for 1705.* Philadelphia, 1704.

Thomas, Gabriel. *History of Pennsylvania and West-Jersey.* London, 1698.

Thompson, Mark. *The Contest for the Delaware Valley.* Baton Rouge: Louisiana State University Press, 2013.

Thumb, Thomas. *The Monster of Monsters.* Boston, 1754.

Tomlin, T. J. *A Divinity for all Persuasions: Almanacs and Early American Religious Life.* New York: Oxford University Press, 2014.

Tomlin, T. J. "'Astrology's from Heaven not Hell': The Religious Significance of Early American Almanacs." *Early American Studies* 8:2 (2010): 287–321.

Tribble, Scott. *A Colossal Hoax: The Giant from Cardiff that Fooled America.* Lanham, MD: Rowan & Littlefield, 2008.

Versluis, Arthur. *The Esoteric Origins of the American Renaissance.* New York: Oxford University Press, 2001.

Versluis, Arthur. *Wisdom's Children: A Christian Esoteric Tradition.* Albany: State University of New York Press, 1999.

Wacker, Peter O. *Land and People: A Cultural Geography of Preindustrial New Jersey: Origins and Settlement Patterns.* New Brunswick, NJ: Rutgers University Press, 1975.

Watkins, John Elfreth. "Demon of the Pines." *Evening Star* (Washington, DC), September 2, 1905.

Weinberger, Jerry. *Benjamin Franklin Unmasked: On the Unity of His Moral, Religious, and Political Thought.* Lawrence: University of Kansas Press, 2005.

Weslager, C. A. *The Delaware Indians: A History.* New Brunswick, NJ: Rutgers University Press, 1972.

Widmer, Kemble. *The Geology and Geography of New Jersey.* Princeton, NJ: D. Van Nostrand, 1964.

Wilding, Nick. "The Return of Thomas Salusbury's Life of Galileo." *British Journal for the History of Science* 41:2 (2008).

Winick, Stephen D. "Tales of the Jersey Devil." Botkin Archives, American Folklore Center, Library of Congress, 2005.

Winship, Michael. *Making Heretics: Militant Protestantism and Free Grace in Massachusetts, 1636–1641.* Princeton, NJ: Princeton University Press, 2002.

WPA Guide to 1930s New Jersey. New York: Viking Press, 1939.

Zeisberger, David. In *History of the North American Indians,* edited by Archer Hulbert and William F. Schwarze. Cincinnati: Ohio Archaeological and Historical Society, 1910.

Index

Page numbers in *italics* indicate illustrations.